ender

11

Gender and Policing

Comparative Perspectives

Jennifer Brown
and
Frances Heidensohn

First Published in Great Britain 2000 by
MACMILLAN PRESS LTD
Houndmills, Basingstoke, Hampshire RG21 6XS and London
Companies and representatives throughout the world

A catalogue record for this book is available from the British
Library

ISBN: 0-333-73061-5 paperback
ISBN: 0-333-73060-7 hardback

 First published in the United States of America 2000 by
ST. MARTIN'S PRESS, LLC,
Scholarly and Reference Division,
175 Fifth Avenue,
New York, N. Y. 10010

ISBN: 0-312-23308-6

Library of Congress Cataloging-in-Publication Data
Brown, Jennifer M.
Gender and policing: comparative perspectives/Jennifer Brown and Frances
Heidensohn. p. cm.
Includes bibliographical references and index.
ISBN 0-312-23308-6 (cloth)
1. Policewomen. 2. Sex role in the work environment. 3. Law enforcement.
I. Heidensohn, Frances. II. Title.
HV8023.B76 2000
363.2'082—dc21

99-086555

This book is printed on paper suitable for recycling and made from fully managed
and sustained forest sources.

10   9   8   7   6   5   4   3   2   1
09   08   07   06   05   04   03   02   01   00

Printed in China

To Elaine and to Martin

Contents

Acknowledgements

This book could not have been written without the help and enthusiasm of many people. We first wish to thank those whom we cannot name, the women who participated in the surveys and interviews. They entrusted us with their stories to which we hope we have done justice.

The interviews were carried out by us (FH) and (JB) and by Nikki Batten, Jane Creaton and Marisa Silvestri whose energy and enthusiasm contributed to the success of the project. Bernadette Pica provided research assistance in handling the quantitative analysis. Her infectious curiosity acted as a spur to extract more out of the data.

We both greatly enjoyed the work undertaken for this book which has taken us to unexpected places and events. This included several libraries. In particular, the documentation centre of the ENP, the Police Staff College library at Bramshill, the Public Record Office, the Fawcett Library, the library at the Imperial War Museum, the Glasgow Women's Library, the Scottish Police College library, the Northern Ireland Office, the Metropolitan Police Museum, The Mitchell Library in Glasgow. Staff were unfailingly kind, courteous and patient when unearthing little-used and often dusty documents.

Specific individuals who gave us their time and views on earlier drafts of chapters include Dorothy Schulz, Rebecca Horn, and Joan Lock. We are extremely grateful for their helpful comments and enthusiastic support for the book.

We would also like to acknowledge two inspirational women who wrote earlier histories of women in policing and whose work provided the starting point for our own researches, Sandra Jones and Susan Martin.

The organizers of the conferences where we were able to gather our empirical data greatly facilitated this project. We thank

Caroline Williamson (West Midlands Police), Anita Hazenberg (ENP) and Melinda Tynan (New South Wales Police).

Thanks too go to Nigel Woodger, who provided technical expertize for production of the illustrations.

Frances Heidensohn would particularly like to pay tribute to the patience and support shown by Jennifer Brown to a co-author who was slowed down by various events and distractions during the course of this project.

The writing of the book is our responsibility as are any of its shortcomings. What strengths it may have are in no small part due to contributions offered by colleagues and the legion of anonymous participants in our survey.

JENNIFER BROWN
FRANCES HEIDENSOHN

1

Introduction: Setting the Scene

Introduction

This book is an ambitious project, both in range and scope. It represents a development and an integration of research into women in policing which both of us from our respective disciplines of psychology (JB) and criminology (FH) had been pursuing for a number of years. Not a topic to attract significant funding, an international comparison of policewomen required considerable effort and ingenuity to obtain the necessary resources and collect appropriate source materials to conduct the research. We had a number of practical and conceptual difficulties to overcome including access to information and informants, accommodating psychological and criminological principles of research, contextualizing the study, layering our levels of analysis and melding our different methodological approaches. This introductory chapter explains why we think this has been a worthwhile enterprise, outlines our conceptual approach, documents the ways in which we overcome the methodological difficulties, and lays out the questions for which we sought answers.

Rationale

Not until Susan Martin's ground breaking work in the late 1970s had there been a serious academic study on the role and experiences of women police officers (Martin 1979). Before this, there had been some published autobiographical accounts or biographies of women officers (for example, Allen 1925; Wyles 1951) which conform to the celebratory phase of police research outlined by Reiner

(1992). Later research, often by serving or former policewomen, merges Reiner's consensus and conflictual phases of research, in that some work sought to promote the heroic activities of women officers whilst others were more critical of the limits placed on women in the police (for example, Lock 1979; Lucas 1986). Post equality legislation, there was a blossoming of research in the United States (see Lunneborg 1989 for a review); a steady growth in studies from Britain dating from Jones (1986) (see Heidensohn 1992 for a review); an emergence of research from Australia (for example, Prenzler 1994, 1996, 1998; Wimshurst 1995; Chan 1996, 1997) and a smattering of one-off investigations such as John Brewer's analysis of women in the Royal Ulster Constabulary (Brewer 1991a) and Aleem on women police in India (Aleem 1989). In addition, some cross-cultural analyses have been attempted between the United States of America and the United Kingdom (Heidensohn 1992) and within Europe (Brown 1997). Thus, not quite a canon but certainly a respectable corpus of work now exists on police women that spans a range of topics such as evaluation of women's effectiveness as police officers, their motivation, stress, job satisfaction, coping, discriminatory experiences, histories and cross-cultural comparison. So why this book?

At a time when academic activity, certainly in the United States and United Kingdom, is dominated by the requirements of tenure track and research assessment exercises, it is somewhat novel to be able to undertake a piece of work because it held intrinsic scholarly interest for us both. Gender issues are a relative latecomer to the field of criminal justice studies and examination of women's involvement in policing permitted us to become immersed in fascinating personal stories and to uncover lost texts that charted the small victories won by individuals developing women's contribution to and changing practice in law enforcement worldwide. It became apparent that when laid out, these parallel histories were not only common but seemingly had to be repeated by women pioneers in whatever police jurisdiction they were struggling to enter. Not only did new issues emerge, but further delving allowed us to understand more about how and why resistance to women police officers arose and is sustained across time and cultures. This constituted a 're-remembering' of the lost or invisible pioneers and their present day contemporaries in order to provide a realistic assessment of their influence on policing.

Policing has experienced something of a crisis worldwide. With Commissions of Inquiry into excessive use of force in the United States, corruption scandals in Australia, racial tensions in Britain, and sex crimes in Belgium, examination of police organizations through a gender looking-glass reveals the inadequacies of explanatory models provided by contemporary research approaches which, by and large, ignore the gender dimension. We are able to extend issues related to the police occupational culture and show how modern policing policies such as zero tolerance look when examined through our particular looking-glass.

Cross-cultural work on policing has largely developed by comparing models of policing dominated by men. Analytical frameworks and conceptual tools were fashioned accordingly. By putting women into the frame, we seek to finesse and/or customize new conceptualizations. In particular, we use time and numbers (of women officers) as analytical tools to complement cross-cultural comparison. This allowed us some insights into the repetitive cycles of experience that women in different jurisdictions encountered in their efforts to enter and make progress. We also offer a policing typology that we hope will stimulate some debate about ways of thinking about and assessing police behaviour and policing functions.

There has been relatively little multi-disciplinary collaboration that tackles research into policing. Reiner's (1992) wide ranging overview of research into policing within the United Kingdom drew largely on sociological and criminological scholarship and made little mention of psychological contributions. Our collaboration attempts to bridge the disciplinary divide by offering a synthesis of collectivist and individual standpoints. We contextualize policing and explore structural features of police organizations. We also locate women within these by examining psychological factors such as their coping strategies and personal self efficacy.

The task itself posed considerable methodological challenges, not least access to both information and informants. Police organizations have been reluctant to permit open access for research purposes and the logistics of negotiating permissions with different countries seemed daunting – hence our use of international conferences as our research site to conduct surveys and interviews. By taking a multi-method approach, we seek to contribute not only to research into policing but, hopefully, wider application to other difficult research topics. Thus, we undertook a questionnaire survey and conducted individual and group interviews. We also made use of quantitative and qualitative methods of analysis. This involved some statistical procedures to try and establish the pattern of general trends and these are presented in Chapter 5 outlining the results of the survey. We also employed two types of qualitative analysis. The first, presented in Chapter 3, is a discourse analysis of historical materials and artefacts which attempts not just to look at language and symbols but argues that these themselves are constructs of social reality. There are the problems of language and translation in documentary material. We used illustrative material such as cartoons to help transcend linguistic boundaries. Through discourse analysis, we looked at the constructive process and traced the social and psychological implications for the working lives of police women. Our interview material was analysed by drawing upon the concepts derived from Heidensohn's grounded theory analysis of American and British policewomen (Heidensohn 1992).

There is also the matter of social justice. Women found gaining access to law-enforcement agencies a struggle. Their numbers in the police are still lamentably low. Discrimination and sexual harassment persist. Women's impact on the law and order agenda and styles of policing are limited. We wished to explore these issues in the wider context of a cross-cultural frame to look for regularities and explanations.

Working model

In undertaking this research, we considered as three axes underpinning our analysis: structural relations (that is, time and numbers); conceptual content (that is, Heidensohn's 1992 categories and psychological processes); cross-cultural comparison (that is, United Kingdom, United States, Australia, Europe and Africa).

Structural dimensions

Time

Time may be factored into social science research in a variety of ways, although much scholarly activity tends to operate within contemporary snapshots. Prospective studies attempt to establish

Figure 1 Analytical framework

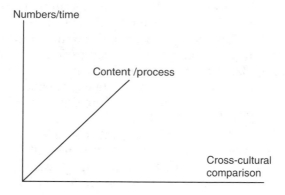

a large database and track cohorts across time in order to identify significant factors in terms of a specified phenomenon. The work of David Farrington and colleagues in their studies of juvenile delinquency is a classic example of studies of this type. Retrospective analyses are more unusual. Psychologists in particular have avoided using retrospective analyses in research, largely because of the inaccessibility of materials and difficulties in establishing reliability (Chase 1995, p. 315). Chase, however, provides a strong case for historically grounded psychological research, suggesting that this can aid the process of hypothesis generating and testing as well as illustrating the operation of psychological processes. In terms of the subject of our analyses, we take a position adopted by Halford, Savage and Witz (1997, p. 19) that 'historically established modes [of behaviour] are vitally important in shaping current activities'. They argue that present organizational structures, practices and culture are the devices by which past forms of agency have been stored and sedimented such that they can be maintained and reactivated. We sought to salvage past practices and culture within police organizations in order to obtain some purchase on present attitudes towards women police officers that contribute to the continued presence of discriminatory behaviour. It was notions of the durability of these attitudes that we were after as well as their reflexivity that might account for their persistence and apparent resistance to change.

Police forces vary considerably in terms of the dates at which women were recruited. There was a time lag in most forces in terms of the original inception of the force and the entry of women. Martin (1979) and Heidensohn (1992) draw a time line that describes the history of US and UK women's entry and progression within policing. Heidensohn extended Martin's two-stage model to identify key landmarks which include the appointment of the first women police officers; a latency period in which women officers consolidated their separatist roles in dealing with women and children; the formulation and enactment of equality legislation and disbanding of the separate women's departments. We suggest three broad time bands when women entered: the early 1900s to World War II (which we call the elders period); post-Second World War to about 1960s; (which we call seasoned) and a modern period beginning in the 1970s to the present (which we call fledgling).

1900s to World War II (elders)
Nurse Henriette Arendt was the first woman appointed by the Stuttgart police to assist with medical investigations and taking care of women in prison (Hazenberg and Ormiston 1995). From 1908 to 1924, about sixty towns in Germany followed this pattern. Segrave (1995) notes that they had no training, powers of arrest and their role was regarded as experimental. The first contingent of women uniformed police was in Cologne in 1923 introduced to help stop the spreading of venereal disease amongst the occupying troops. During the Second-World War years, women who worked for the secret police in Germany, were somewhat demonized. The women Gestapo agents, described as 'gaunt, forbidding, big of limb, big of muscle, cruel, hard faced creatures,' were 'fiends who surpass the men in brutality and in their inhumane behaviour ... Women were organised to accomplish tasks that even the most brutalised German men would have hesitated to undertake' (Baxter 1943, p. 16). Hazenberg and Ormiston (1995) note that after World War II Germany was divided into four zones and policing conducted in the manner of the occupying countries, that is, United States, Britain, France and USSR. By 1974 the separate women's departments were integrated with the criminal police. However it was not until the 1970s that the Minister of the Interior allowed women to join the uniformed police in Germany. Hazenberg and Ormiston (1995, p. 39) conclude: 'Previously those in authority had held the view that the work of the uniformed police was too physically demanding for women. This stereotyping meant that it took rather a long time

before the anti-discrimination act, already set out in the basic law, was finally put into practice in the police service.'

Agda Halldin was the first Swedish woman police officer joining the Stockholm Police in 1908 (Hazenberg and Ormiston 1995). She and her contemporaries were trained nurses and were employed as police sisters guarding, searching and taking care of women and children who had been taken to police stations. Women were not uniformed until 1958. Hazenberg and Ormiston (1995) describe the police strategic plan for personnel matters which was established in 1991 which developed policy for recruitment, education, career planning and training.

The first Dutch policewoman, Dina Samson, entered the Rotterdam Municipal Police in 1911 (Hazenberg and Ormiston 1995). Other cities followed this example following pressure from women's groups about the policing of sexual offences. It was not until 1953 that three women began work as uniformed police officers. In 1971 the first women were allowed to enter the Dutch Police Academy to train as senior officers. As late as 1979, 57 per cent of police forces in the Netherlands had no women operational police officers. In 1983 the Ministry of the Interior set up an equality working group which resulted in modifications in entrance tests and selection criteria for women officers. By 1990 a national Police Equal Opportunities Policy was produced.

French women began to make inroads into the non-military police in 1914 when the Prefet de Police for Paris employed 12 typists (Dene 1992, p. 238). However it was not until 1935 that another Prefet employed two women to assist in Paris' juvenile bureau. These first policewomen wore uniform and came under the direction of the Direction Generale de la Police Municipale en Paris. During the Second World War, possibly because of the German occupation, women's role within the police did not develop. Although the creation of Corps des Serveillantes Auxilliaires de Police in 1943 did create some opportunities for women. Rinsema (1996, p. 24) notes that equality legislation in France was enacted after the Second World War but that exceptions were made if the nature of the work justified this remaining segregated, arguments deployed by the French police. It was to be European legislation that outlawed exclusive recruitment and treatment of policewomen during the 1970s and 1980s. Although in the 1960s women had been integrated into the Corps des Policiers en Civil, it was not until 1968 that women received any real recognition albeit in principally

traditional domains: child protection work, regulation of prostitution and administrative duties. Thus it was not until 1983 that career
opportunities were really opened up to French policewomen in the
national police (Maniloff 1998). By 1993 women constituted 6.4 per
cent of the national police. Rinsema (1996, p. 26) concludes, for
women in the French police forces: 'It has become clear that there
used to be quite a number of legal impediments preventing women
to gain a place within the national police . . . In addition things were
not exactly made easy for women. For example, the police stations
were not suitable for women and neither were the uniforms.'

In 1915, New South Wales Police advertised two positions for
female officers and about 500 women applied. Two applicants,
Lillian Armfield and Maud Rhodes were chosen and sworn in as
probationary special constables (Tynan 1995). In the same year
Kate Cocks joined the South Australian Police. Two years later,
in 1917, Helen Blanche Dugdale was appointed to the police in
Western Australia and Miss Connors and Beers joined as 'police
agents' in Victoria. Their duties were to track persons suspected of
decoying girls for prostitution, visit railway stations and wharfs to
give advice to the unwary, patrol slum areas and keep an eye on
houses of ill repute. Women did not join the Northern Territory
Police until 1961. The Equal Opportunity Act of 1978 saw the
integration of policewomen and they were able to transfer to general
duties or other areas of work for which they held appropriate
qualifications.

In 1910, women entered policing in the United States and in
Britain around the time of the First World War (Heidensohn
1992; Schulz 1995a) as a consequence of the agitation of moral
reform and social hygiene movements. They too were restricted
within policewomen's departments. A major difference between
British and American pioneer policewomen was their attitudes
towards uniform with the latter resisting this until the 1960s. Equality legislation in 1964 and 1975 respectively heralded the demise of
the policewomen's departments and the integration of women.

Entry of women in policing in Canada also dates from 1910
although the policewomen were selected on different criteria to
men and limited to working with women, children and typewriters
(Walker 1993). As in Europe and North America, Canadian policewomen remained in these restricted roles until Human Rights legislation led to 'a dramatic expansion' in the recruitment of women
(Walker 1993: 1). The Royal Canadian Mounted Police (RCMP)

organizations has an impact on opportunities for advancement. Halford, Savage and Witz (1997, p. 7) summarizes Kanter's proposition as follows. To prosper, organizations require good communications and reduction of uncertainties. In order to maximize these features there is a tendency to appoint similar individuals to senior positions. Thus, in organizations which have been historically male dominated, managers will be appointed who share common features. This sustains male hierarchies, not through exercise of gender preferences but through choice of sameness or 'homosociability'. This process excludes those who are different – women, ethnic minorities, homosexuals – from upward mobility and sets up a cycle of discouragement and lowered motivation which inhibits performance, reduces organizational recognition and limits chances of advancement. Critical to this argument are the relative proportions of men and women in the workplace. Kanter (1977) proposes that if a minority group is below 15 per cent, individuals are likely to be highly visible, attract a disproportionate share of attention and are susceptible to stress as a consequence of dysfunctional work-performance pressures due to this untoward attention. Individuals in this situation are called 'tokens'. Tokens face isolation because they are different and they are subjected to distorted perceptions and stereotyping by the majority. Thus they become mistake-avoidance sensitive, have an exaggerated fear of failure at important tasks or key events, and worry about retaliation by envious dominant group members (Wersch 1998, p. 52). For women, the work culture thus advances unsavoury images of femininity which Kanter describes as the little sister (dependent and incompetent) seductress (incompetent and flirtatious) iron maiden (competent and hard) the mother (competent at looking after men's emotions but nagging).

Kanter's answer to these problems is to create gender balance which will 'burcaucratise' out inequalities. However, Halford, Savage and Witz (1997, p. 9) argue that this is an unsustainably optimistic prediction because organizations reflect specifically male values and modes of behaviour. It follows that even if more women were appointed to senior positions, the organization will not lose its male characteristics. They argue (p. 10) that women will be co-opted into the male culture, that they will still be marked out from men and their organizational power undermined. This is an argument that resonates with Daly's position with respect to the judiciary. She proposes (Daly 1989, p. 22) that within the dispensation of justice,

were rather late in admitting women to serve as police officers. Women had been employed as matrons since 1892, and later women filled civilian support roles such as fingerprint or laboratory technicians *(RCMP Gazette,* vol, 56, no. 9, 1994*)*. The first troop of female regular officers was not recruited until 1974. Thus it was not until 1981 that a women achieved a supervisory rank, 1990 a commander rank and 1994 a commissioner rank.

Post-Second World War (seasoned)

Rinsema (1996) notes that equal opportunities in public service in Denmark was established by law in 1920 but that the Police Service was exempted. A few female officers were employed to deal with sexual offences. There were only 28 women employed in the Danish Police by 1948. It was not until 1977 that women were afforded equal access to all types of police work and ranks. Danish police are armed but it was only relatively recently that women were issued with the same weapons as their male colleagues. Promotion is after eight years of service (which appears to be indirectly discriminating to women) because of family commitments.

Hazenberg and Ormiston (1995) note that the first intake of women into the Garda Siochana was 1959 yet by the end of World War I, there were women in the Royal Irish Constabulary to deal with wayward girls but who had no powers of arrest and were not paid from police funds *(Policewomen's Review* 1931). Two policewomen transferred to the RUC in 1922 although they were referred to as matrons (Cameron 1993). Brewer (1991a) states that women were first recruited into the RUC in 1944 and restricted to Belfast and Derry to deal exclusively with women and children. The Garda Siochana was exempted from the Employment Equality Act of 1977 until it was obliged to comply through the enactment of an EC Directive. Equal pay for women in the Garda Siochana followed successful litigation initiated on behalf of women sergeants who until then received a third less pay than their male counterparts. Under Sir Kenneth Newman, the RUC operated a modified role for policewomen in which they performed all duties except those of a secure nature involving firearms. Brewer (1991b, p. 236) describes men's perception of women police as follows: 'women have an instinct for tidiness which makes them good administrators; frequently they were described as being suited to dealing with child and female offences because of their more compassionate natures'. The attitudes of the force to its women officers is neatly encapsulated in the Chief Constable's statement when defending the RUC against a sex discrimination challenge by a woman reservist.

> The Chief Constable considers that if women officers were armed, it would increase the risk that they might become targets for assassination, that armed women officers would be less effective in areas for which women are 'better suited' such as welfare work dealing with families and children, and that if women were to carry fire-arms it would be regarded by the public as a much greater departure from the ideal of an unarmed police force (Johnston vs Chief Constable of the Royal Ulster Constabulary 1986).

Despite the judgement being found for the appellant, it was not until 1993 that the distinction between men and women RUC officers with respect to firearms was finally removed (*Police Review* 1993).

Nineteen women began work for the Hungarian Police based at Headquarters, Budapest in 1946. This was as a result of displaced and homeless children in the aftermath of World War II (Hazenberg and Ormiston 1995). Women were employed in a social work function to collect children and find homes for them. The Hungarian Police does not have a written equal opportunities policy or grievance procedure and part-time working is not possible for operational policewomen. Currently most policewomen work in public safety or public administration (Sarkozi 1994).

Cherrett (1990) notes that the need for policewomen in New Zealand was discussed in 1914 when early feminists lobbied the Government to employ women on a full-time basis. Women were not appointed until 1941 when 12 were personally selected by the Commissioner and posted to Auckland, Wellington, Christchurch and Dunedin. Unsure what to do with the new appointees, he gave the women typing and other clerical duties. New Zealand policewomen were not issued with a uniform until 1952. Early operational duties included arrest of vagrant women and policing of illegal abortions. Conditions and duties changed somewhat spasmodically and their duties were restricted until the 1960s when Commissioner Spencer introduced equal pay and disbanded the separate women's divisions. However, women were not truly integrated until 1973 with the restatement of equality policies by Commissioner Sharp.

Post-1970s (fledgling)

Women did not enter policing in the African subcontinent until the 1950s and 60s. Igbinovia (1987, p. 32) notes that the women's

branch of the police was first formed in Ghana in 1952, in Nigeria in 1955 and in Kenya in 1965. Women first entered the police service in Botswana in 1971. By 1998, 394 women served out of a total of 5221 officers (7.5 per cent) and, as a percentage of women 26 per cent held a supervisory rank. Interestingly, this was the same percentage as women serving in England and Wales before the 1975 Sex Discrimination Act. By 1978, Egypt, Mauritania and Senegal still did not employ any policewomen. It is the contention of Igbinovia (1987) that Eurocentric prejudices were a factor in the late employment of women officers in police forces in Africa. Not only did African countries inherit sex discrimination from European models of law enforcement, but administrators in new African nations maintained bias against policewomen. This was especially the case in French Colonial Africa since policewomen in the home country were, according to Igbinovia (1987, p. 33) 'nothing better than meter maids without any police power or authority'.

The gendarmeries of Europe tended to be late in their admittance of women. In Spain there are four types of police: national; military (Civil Guard); municipal; and police forces of 17 autonomous regions. Rinsema (1996) notes that women were admitted to the Spanish police in the 1970s. Special units of women were formed and they were employed in research support for narcotics and other special criminal squads. In 1977, women were eligible for selection to the police academy. In 1983 restrictions were lifted and women had the same rights and duties as men.

The first 20 women cadets were recruited into the Luxembourg Gendarmerie in 1979; and it only became possible for women to join the Belgian Gendarmerie in 1975 because of an amendment to the law. However it was not until 1981 that the first woman was recruited. Since the demilitarization of the Belgian Gendarmerie the number of women are increasing due to an affirmative action programme.

Numbers

Research into the position and experience of women police officers has drawn on the theoretical work of Rosabeth Kanter (Ott 1989; Martin 1989b; Brown 1998; Wertsch 1998: Wimshurst 1995). Kanter's thesis proposes that distortions in the gender balance

certain relations are presumed, maintained and reproduced in ways that victimize the least powerful (women, children and ethnic minorities). So as Miller (1998, p. 100) concludes, 'merely adding more female judges to the bench or further changing the system ... [will] not necessarily change currently existing legal or criminal justice system practice.' Chan (1996, p. 131) proposes that reform of the police informal culture in terms of procedural rule tightening alone is insufficient to eliminate discrimination because without changes within the criminal justice system and wider societal environments, police practice 'may revert to old dispositions.' This suggests that it is not enough to increase numbers to achieve a transformation of the prevailing values and behaviours of the dominant (white male) group within the police.

This book then attempts to locate policewomen in their historical context and to deconstruct themes associated with women's entry into policing. We chart in Chapter 2, policewomen's progress in breaking the mould, and disinter the historical trace elements characterizing their developmental progress. It is from an historical analysis that we locate the inhibitions that will be shown to continue to impact women police officers. Since the bedrock of opposition to women as police officers relates to their physiques and sexuality, we centre analyses around notions of the body as manifest in drawings and cartoons as well as verbal materials. This approach represents a novel method as well as synthesizing analytical frames used by previous reviewers of police in general and of women police in particular.

Content/processes

Concepts within our analytical framework were derived from Heidensohn's (1992) grounded theory analysis of American and British policewomen. Brown (1997) demonstrated the utility of employing Heidensohn's working themes in providing a comparative analysis of European policewomen's experiences. These are: 'pioneering' and 'mission' used to review policewomen in their historical setting; 'working with partners', 'professionalism' and 'transformational scenes' allow comparison of working practices; 'soft cops', 'female cop culture' and 'top cops' are drawn together under the general heading of women's coping adaptations and policing style.

Sexism

Sex and sexism, either implicit or explicit, are never very far away when it comes to discussing policewomen. Concerns about female sexuality, its institutional control through marriage or formal organizational structures (and informally through male violence and harassment) and the consequent demarcation into male and female roles and distribution of power, have been articulated by Halford, Savage and Witz (1997). They make three particularly important points applicable to our analysis of policewomen: first, as previously mentioned, historically established modes are vitally important in understanding current behaviour (p. 19); secondly, women's subordination at work is eroticized or sexualized (p. 21) and control is exercised through pleasure as well as harassment; thirdly, the body itself is a significant component of discourses around gender and sexuality in organizations (p. 27). They argue that both socially constructed aspects of sexuality (sexuality paradigm) and biological aspects of women's (and men's) bodies (gender paradigm) are employed as devices to subordinate women and justify their exclusions from specific roles and seniority in organizations. Origins of attitudes towards policewomen can be found historically in stereotypic mythology about the 'good' woman, compliant and ignorant or naive about sex other than that which is necessary for child bearing, who is protected by her father then husband and the 'bad' woman who understands sex only too well and whose ways are that of all flesh leading to depravity. The modern version of this myth relates to notions that sexually active women having multiple partners are illicit, promiscuous and thus compromised whilst the equivalent male is knowledgeable, experienced and thus desirable. The language used to describe both has negative connotations for women and positive for men: 'stud' suggests superiority of breeding potential whilst 'bike' (a slang term for a sexually available woman) indicates something rather less glamorous and somewhat more disposable.

Gender relations are accentuated in policing which is one of the quintessentially male occupations where men's ascendancy to both define control and own the methods of control were assured until the advent of women police. This ascendancy was not to be yielded easily. The content of objections to women police officers and the language employed when expressing these objections alternates between needing to protect 'good' women from the seamier side of life and fear that 'bad' women will contaminate policing and lead policemen astray. Policewoman is the ultimate oxymoron. Policing is about conserving the *status quo*, separating the good from the bad and invoking compliance by the legitimate use of force. On the one hand, to be a police officer requires knowing about the bad but not being corrupted by it. For women knowing about the bad is tantamount to being bad. On the other hand, police officers may be required to intervene physically, thought to be unproblematic for men but felt to be entirely unsuitable for women.

Harassment

Sexual harassment can be considered as part of the continuum of violence against women. Common themes emerge when considering women's experience of rape, domestic violence and sexual harassment in terms of attitudes towards victims, symptoms suffered, coping strategies employed and inclination to lodge a formal complaint and have been imbedded in notions that violence is the exercise by men of control over women (Stanko 1985; Heidensohn 1992). The latter argues that men restrict and limit women's scope and horizons in:

- families by loading domestic tasks onto women or by threatening or perpetrating violence on them;
- the media by perpetuating models for women to be 'good' whilst making no similar claims to influence the behaviour of men;
- the criminal justice system which fails to recognize violence against women as a crime and fails to punish perpetrators.

Men's violence, it is claimed, is commonly assumed to be normal and obscured behind a wall of accepted behaviour (Stanko 1985, p. 60). Janoff-Bulman (1988), whilst conceding psychological consequences, proposes that violence involves physical force with the intent to harm and that 'the plight of the victim...is generally understood in terms of physical violation' (p. 101). Stanko (1992), however, argues for a much broader definition in that violence is about inflicting emotional, psychological, sexual, physical and/or material harm. This not only expands notions of violence beyond the physical, but also extends the location of violence. Kennedy

(1993), for example, discusses the public/private dichotomy in which behaviours occurring within the home were said to constitute private concerns and by implication not an issue requiring the intervention of the law. A man beating his wife is a private trouble, an explanation also advanced for the occurrence of sexual harassment (Hoffman 1986).

Mezey and Rubenstein (1992) suggest that work, like home, can be represented as a caring, self-contained unit. Both have hierarchical structures with unwritten rules and codes of conduct, usually defined by the more powerful members. The less powerful members are often passive and dependent performing servicing functions in exchange for care and protection. In many families and workplaces, the most powerful tend to be men. Less powerful members, usually women, who 'cause trouble' tend to be isolated and frequently scapegoated as a mechanism to preserve the power relationships. Power relationships are an issue in sexual harassment. The harasser is often the women's boss. As employees are dependent on their job for their livelihood, psychological well-being and self-esteem, there seems little option but to stay. A woman's attempts to define violent behaviour as unacceptable has connotations of her inviting or causing her own harm. In other words, women are held responsible for their own victimization. Siegal (1992) compares cultural mythologies that seek to blame women for being raped or battered. These include beliefs that 'women ask for it'; 'women say no when they mean yes' and that women's narratives about violence are unreliable. She argues that these attributions can also be found amongst the mythologies surrounding the experience of sexual harassment.

Incidence of sexual harassment is difficult to pinpoint. Stockdale (1991) reports that estimates ranging from 25 to 90 per cent of women at work experience sexual harassment. Salisbury *et al.* (1986) suggest that fewer than one in ten women actually file a formal complaint. They fail to do so because of fear of retaliation, loss of privacy and self-blame. MacKinnon (1995) notes that most victims of sexual harassment never file complaints because they feel ashamed. MacKinnon also observes (p. 305) 'a woman's word, even if believed was legally insufficient, even if the man had nothing to put against it other than his word and the plaintiff's burden of proof'.

Fiske (1991) outlined characteristics of organizations in which discrimination and harassment were likely to occur. These included the following: minority groups constituting less than 20 per cent of the workforce; percentage of managers from minority groups is lower than represented percentage in the workforce; uneven distribution of minorities in the full range of departments or specialism; presence of sexually explicit materials in the workforce; tolerance of obscene or profane language in the workforce; lone presence of minorities in organizational locations. By and large, these features are all present in police organizations.

Coping strategies

Coping with adverse circumstances have been categorized as problem-focused or emotion-focused strategies. Wilkinson and Campbell (1997, p. 205) explain these as follows. Problem-focused strategies attempt to confront problems directly and deal with the demands of the situation itself. This often involves problem-solving and may include self-directed strategies, seeking help from others or trying to change the situation (for example, by appealing to the union). Emotion-focused strategies are aimed more at managing the anxiety generated by the situation. This may include venting anger, denial of the external reality when it is too unpleasant, or rationalizing by assigning some apparently logical or socially desirable interpretation to events or behavior.

Coping in work environments has been examined in relation to women managing in non-traditional careers (Neville and Schlecker 1988) in terms of self-efficacy and assertiveness. They found that women having high levels of self-efficacy and assertiveness were associated with willingness to make career choices in non-traditional occupations. They argue that it follows that increasing both through training is likely to help women in seeking and succeeding in non-traditional occupations. However, in male dominated professions such as policing it still seems that women not only have a lower sense of self-efficacy than policemen but also assume that their male counterparts perceive this to be so (Singer and Love 1988). These researchers were able to show that self-efficacy had no bearing on the officer's (male or female) psychological well-being, job satisfaction or job involvement. We explore issues of self-efficacy in Chapter 5 when presenting the results of our survey data.

Self-efficacy

Given the strong occupational cultural ethos of the police, the concept of self-efficacy is helpful when attempting to assess the relative influences an individual woman may have in managing her career, working and personal relationships. Notions of self-efficacy derive from work by Bandura (1995). He argues that people strive to exercise control over their lives in order to realize desired futures and to forestall undesirable ones. Self-efficacy is defined (p. 2) as 'beliefs in one's capabilities to organize and execute the courses of action required to manage prospective situations.' There are said to be four main influences determining levels of self-efficacy: mastery influences in which success builds confidence although self-efficacy can emerge more strongly if success is achieved after a set-back; vicarious experience in which similar people being seen to succeed by perseverance raises beliefs that the individual too can succeed; social persuasion whereby people are verbally persuaded that they possess the capabilities to master activities (those who are persuaded they lack capability tend to avoid challenging activities and often give up in the face of difficulties); physiological and emotional states such as stress reactions can signal vulnerability and lead to poor performance. Breakwell (1992, p. 35) points out that self-efficacy has less to do with the actual outcomes, either positive or negative, but with whether or not people believe that they can behave in a certain way and as such 'is the foundation stone of personal agency'. Thus when women are faced with the difficult task of managing a taxing environment such as that of the police, those who harbour a low sense of self-efficacy are likely to lower their aspirations, and the quality of their performance and achievement are likely to decline correspondingly. Those with a stronger sense of self-efficacy are likely to take on problematic situations and have a stronger commitment to achieving their goals. Breakwell (1992) reports results of a study of 15/16 year olds and 17/18 year olds and found, in terms of attitudes towards work, that the stronger the young people's feelings of incompetence are, the greater the likelihood of young women accepting traditional subordinate sex roles and of young men attempting to keep women in those subordinate roles. Lent and Brown (1996) argue that work environments can provide resources or create hardship that facilitates or inhibits a sense of self-efficacy. Thus, it is possible that the police culture might overwhelm any sense of personal self-efficacy in women and actively cultivate a sense of incompetence, placing the onus of failure on the individual rather than on adverse organizational practices.

Cross-cultural comparison

Whilst time might allow us to account for the durability of attitudes towards women in the police, cross-cultural comparison assists us in the task of establishing the regularity, and possibly, the universality of experience. The classic psychological cross-cultural study was by Hofstede (1980) who looked at employee attitudes in a multinational company, later identified as IBM, across 40 different countries. Hofstede used factor analysis of the mean scores aggregated for the 40 countries in the study to distinguish four dimensions which were then used for comparison. One dimension included masculinity–femininity characterized by notions of male models of achievement in terms of recognition and earnings and a more collegiate co-operative style identified as feminine. Hofstede enlarged the data base from the original study and then derived three broad regions into which he pooled countries for further analysis. These then were empirically derived conceptualizations and typologies. In our situation, we have pre-defined measures that we wish to use to compare countries and have developed a conceptually derived typology of police jurisdictions for the purposes of pooling data. Chapter 2 details the derivation of our typology which we are calling cops (the Anglo-American tradition of policing); gendarmes (the European military model); transitionals (those recently democratized policing organizations from Eastern Europe); colonial histories (that is, those police forces whose origins lie with the colonial power of the past).

Hofstede expected that the strong corporate ethos of IBM might override national cultural differences and was surprised to find variation between the countries he studied. Smith and Bond (1993, p. 33) state that 'scientific logic requires that cross-cultural comparisons be made across groups that are equivalent in all respects except for their cultural background.' Like Hofstede, we are assuming that the police occupational culture has some strong unifying themes such as being predominantly male, having a mandate to use reasonable force, engaged in a common mission. We too were expecting similarities across jurisdictions and differences are hypothesized to be due to national cultural variation.

Research questions

What then were our research questions? We were interested to examine the issues of harassment and discrimination and see whether we could establish these as common features of police jurisdictions wherever these may be. We wanted to test the thesis, implicit in Kanter's model, that the balance of gender does have an impact on the type, frequency and severity of discriminatory experiences. What is the lateral and horizontal representation of women in policing? We wondered if we could establish patterns in the pioneer policewomen's experiences that could be linked to the experiences of their present day counterparts. Do such patterns, if found, operate cross-culturally? Would our typology of women police hold up when tested empirically? Could we show that individual characteristics, such as personal self efficacy, overcome the potency of police occupational culture in women's career trajectories? What is the impact of police occupational culture on women officers? What is the impact of women officers on policing? Could we articulate the beginnings of theory to account for differences and similarities between different models of police organization? To answer these questions we needed to:

- access archival materials for the historical dimension of the research
- build a data base with a sufficient number of respondents for some meaningful comparative analyses
- obtain some detailed qualitative data to give substance to the broad themes measured through survey methodologies.

Methodological issues

Problems

Development and progress in research of policewomen's experience have suffered through lack of interest (Heidensohn 1992, p. 80) and, as Lees (1997, p. 177) points out, difficulties in obtaining funding or permission to conduct research into topics such as sexual violence which may cause the police service discomfort. The relatively low numbers of women serving as police officers means recruiting research participants has been difficult (Wertsch 1998, p. 26). This has exacerbated difficulties in establishing either continuity or systematic debate within the research literature. Extension of research into cross-cultural comparisons has been inhibited by absence of source materials (Mawby 1990, p. 192) and shortage of analytical concepts and frameworks (Heidensohn 1992, p. 31). There are many potential pitfalls awaiting the comparative researcher. Heidensohn (1992, p. 199) counsels that: like should be matched with like, differences should not be exaggerated and the innumerable complexities of social and cultural patterns should be recognized. In addition, Smith and Bond (1993) state that if groups in comparative samples are different in ways other than their cultural backgrounds then alternative explanations or plausible rival hypotheses cannot be eliminated. They cite the following problems in conducting cross-cultural comparisons: language problems in translations of questionnaire items; meaning equivalences of terms and concepts (is sexual harassment recognized as the same phenomenon in different cultures?); are different countries similarly experienced in research or opinion polling? Chase (1995) too draws attention to difficulties when conducting research on historical materials: survival of material is sometimes arbitrary and erratic and it is often difficult to demonstrate systematic section of sample materials.

Some of the technical problems in time-based and cross-cultural research can be solved through statistical or methodological techniques. Smith and Bond (1993) recommend that where samples vary, for example, age, statistically partialling out can control for the effects of such variables. Response ranges in questionnaires can be truncated into 'yes' and 'no' answers to avoid confusions or nuances in meaning. They also suggest using imaginative and innovatory approaches as well as careful preparation can off-set other difficulties. Both Smith and Bond (1993) with respect to cross-cultural research and Chase (1995) in terms of time-base research state that use of theory-driven conceptualization enhances the quality of the work and leaves interpretation of results less open to plausible rival hypotheses.

Access to respondents required the employment of some ingenuity. In order to obtain access to law firms to study sex discrimination and harassment experienced by women employees, Jennifer

Pierce disguised her study as an examination of stress to make this more acceptable (Pierce 1995). Heidensohn (1992), Lanier (1996) and Gossett and Williams (1998) adopted a snowball sampling strategy whereby a respondent provided a further contact to participate in the research. This tends to recruit a modest sample and is highly self-selecting. Grant, Garrison and McCormick (1990) and Poole and Pogrebin (1988) contacted delegates attending International Association of Women Police conferences. The advantages of this approach are financial (costs would be prohibitive in attempting to collect data from individual countries), logistical (women serving in a wide range of locations were gathered together) and methodological (administration of a common research instrument). The disadvantages are lack of control over sampling and little claim can be made for the representativeness of the samples.

We rejected the use of deception in our approach to organizations preferring instead a strategy of approaching conference organizers or police forces directly to seek permission to approach delegates for their voluntary participation in a survey. We also made use of direct approaches to delegates in order to recruit participation in a face-to-face interview (for more details see our appendix).

Much of the material used in our analysis is drawn from original source documents. Because we make use of notions of the body as suggested by Halford, Savage and Witz (1997) as a bridge between the sexuality and gender paradigms, we draw on cartoons as source material as these are very explicit rhetorical devices for conveying rather vividly prevailing images of policewomen. We employ analytical procedures adopted from discourse analysis. This is described by Coyle (1995, p. 244) as the analysis of language to show how social realities are constructed. Thus, originators of a commentary such as official reports, letters, speeches and cartoons, select from a range of linguistic or representational resources and use them to create their versions of reality or the world as they would like it to be. The basic assumption of discourse analysis is that linguistic or representational material has an action orientation which seeks to legitimate or question some aspect of social life (Coyle 1995, p. 245). The task for the analyst is to identify what social function is being served and how this is being constructed. We have already identified the social function to be the subject of our close scrutiny of texts: the construction of policewomen's identity. This is achieved by a discussion of both masculinity and femininity within the police and the impact of women's incursion into policing which until the beginning of the twentieth century was entirely a male preserve. Because of the difficulties of accessibility of sources, inherent in cross-cultural analysis of policewomen, much of the original documentation derives from archival material within the United Kingdom. The detailed working through of our themes are grounded in this material. We endeavour to present evidence from other countries where possible to show the universality of the discourses employed with respect to policewomen.

We also make use of statistical analyses in processing the survey data. We employed a multivariate statistical procedure to present empirical evidence supporting our proposed typology. This places us in an interesting position epistemologically. Heidensohn (1992, p. 15) discusses the feministic research tradition as empiricist, standpoint and post modern suggesting that these starting positions affect both the type of questions asked and the methods by which research data are gathered. Empiricists tend towards quantitative approaches, standpoint analysts often employ grounded theory, and discourse analysis would not sit uncomfortably with post modern researchers. We have attempted a multi-method approach which might upset purists from particular positions, and call ourselves eclectic feminists.

2

Comparative Approaches and the Historical Context

Introduction

One of our primary purposes in this book is to explore the experiences of women in policing through international comparison. In later chapters, we do this by analyzing the material we gathered from both a large survey and a series of interviews. We have already outlined some of the key questions for which we sought answers, such as how far policewomen around the world share a single history, how much in common they have today and how far local differences in external or organizational factors have distinctive impact on them. Their own strategies as police officers, as *women* officers and for managing both those roles are also a major focus.

While both the comparative study of criminal justice and the more specific focus on policing seem to be well established, there have been recent contributions to debates in these areas which raise some central issues for this study. Bayley (1999) has offered a robust defence of what he insists should be labelled 'international' or 'cross-national' studies of policing, arguing that it is essential for greater understanding of that phenomenon. He does acknowledge practical problems '[t]he most obvious are language, access and expense' (1999, p. 5), none of which he sees as insuperable (we discuss how we handled these matters in a later chapter). In Bayley's view 'There are four substantial benefits from cross-national study of criminal justice... (1) extending knowledge of alternative possibilities; (2) developing more powerful insights into human behaviour; (3) increasing the likelihood of successful reform and (4) gaining perspective on ourselves as human beings' (1999, p. 6).

In this study we concentrate particularly on the first and third of these; we agree wholeheartedly with Bayley's assertion 'Worldwide description is an essential first step toward the long-term goal of learning about what may work better' (1999, p. 8). Since, as we show in this book, the role of women in policing has strong and distinctive international aspects we believe we can contribute to discussions about how 'research internationally shows whether foreign practice may be successfully imported' (1999, p. 10). The same set of readings of which Bayley's is one contribution includes two chapters by Mawby who outlines further issues in looking at 'policing across the world'. He identifies both advantages and problems in such studies, noting the 'broader perspective' which 'a review of policing in other societies gives' Mawby (1999b, p. 13); but also suggests that Bayley probably understates the difficulties in such research. Mawby himself notes four regular problems 'the availability of valid, reliable and detailed data; second... definitions vary between countries in ways that are not always easily identified and controlled; third is the practical "impossibility of becoming an expert on everywhere"; finally the basis on which to compare and categorize is often complex' (Mawby 1999b, p. 1).

Our approach in this volume is, as far as empirical material goes, quite novel and designed to address some of these problems. As we describe more fully later, we used two sources of direct accounts from modern policewomen: their responses to a survey of their experiences and face-to-face interviews carried out at an international congress. It will become clear that such topics as whether our respondents (all self-identified as serving police officers) were fulfilling policing duties in the sense understood by commentators on policing in the USA or the UK become part of our comparative analysis. Indeed, we have already shown how the entry into and the place of women in policing has been and remains a contested issue. For this reason alone, it is a fascinating topic and also an illuminating one, since debates about gender differences and capacities have thrown such a bright light on central assumptions about policing (Heidensohn 1992). While the collection edited by Mawby (1999a) makes a considerable contribution to this field, one chapter, with Jennifer Brown (*et al.* 1999) as the lead author, considers the issue of policewomen, and other sections largely omit it from discussion.

Comparative research

So that we might pursue our analysis, we looked for ways of ordering our material, of setting it in a framework, to ensure major issues
could be highlighted. Comparative research on policing has several
distinctive advantages: it can offer practical guidance and show
possible pitfalls as far as forms of policy or organization are concerned. The concept of 'zero tolerance' policing, for instance, has
been adopted from experience in New York and advocated as a
solution to crime in Britain (Bratton *et al.* 1997). While policy
transfers may seem attractive, they can be inappropriate: 'Essential
to good comparative work is the realization that elements of one
system cannot necessarily be transferred' (Mawby 1990, p. 11). It is
therefore crucial to place any such translation from one system to
another in context and hence the growth of various theoretical
approaches to comparative work. To cite Mawby once again, with
these come more 'thorough assessment of practices in different
countries and the extent to which they are dependent upon the
wider social, cultural and political structure of the host country'
(*op. cit.*).

There are all kinds of reasons for trying to look at policing across
cultures. The earliest examples of this kind of research provided
handbooks of evidence of both similarity and diversity (Fosdick
1915) in law enforcement agencies. Viewed from one standpoint,
such studies are a subcategory of the general form of comparative
institutional research. Since it is not practically possible to experiment with society by creating laboratory conditions in which all
factors but the key variables are controlled, comparisons of parallel
societies or structures provide the nearest equivalent. Law enforcement is a notable topic here since 'superficially all police departments are the same. They have identical... organizational
philosophies; usually expressed in the form of an aim to prevent
crime and preserve public tranquillity' (McKenzie and Gallagher
1989, p. 3). Undoubtedly the rise in police studies and particularly
their cross-culture variety, have waxed as the police themselves have
been perceived as a *problem*. This is not merely for the pragmatic
reasons noted earlier; it is also because of the growing politicization
of the police in some countries and the issue of accountability
coming to the fore in others (Brewer *et al.* 1996).

Robert Reiner (1992) has charted the developing politics of the
police in Britain and set these alongside the highly charged academic

debates about the origins of the New Police in Britain. He tries to provide a synthesis of these debates; how this history is interpreted can be critical to the way in which the actions of recent and contemporary police are viewed. Thus, even if there was a golden era of policing by consent, there is now no prelapsarian world to which modern police can return. These debates can be further enlightened by comparing the history of police in Britain with those of other countries. The US and Canada make instructive examples. Reiner contrasts evolution in the UK with American 'popular participation in government [which] meant confidence that the police could be entrusted to the political process rather than a tight framework of legal rules and regulations' (Reiner 1986, p. 51). In the US, law officers followed pioneers westward, whereas, as Sewell points out, in Canada 'the police were sent to establish order so that freedom and liberty could be enjoyed' (1986, p. 31). Canada is an instance of a state whose national character was typified by her police force. In a totally different period and place, so was Prussia. Studying these historical cases provides insights not only into their distinctive patterns of law enforcement but also into wider aspects of these societies.

So far we have commented on aspects of a functional approach to comparative policing studies, in short, assuming that law enforcement is typified by its common features and that these arise in characteristic conditions of political development and in response to certain levels of criminality and lawlessness. Another viewpoint, however, might be called diffusionist and stresses the significance of colonialism in the spread of certain types of police organization. Thus in Europe the Code Napoleon was spread across the continent through conquest; the UK and France however exported their own forms and styles of policing to their empires (Brogden 1987).

Another development which has become a major focus of comparative criminological work are 'countries in transition'. Some definitions use this term only to cover former communist states in Europe and the old Soviet Union which share a common heritage and economic status (for a review of this issue, see Zvekic 1998, pp. 4–11). Particular concerns for policy-makers and researchers in these nations are 'corruption in public administration and *the relationship between citizens and the police*' (*op. cit.*, emphasis added). While the International Crime Victim Survey directors choose only to survey this group of nations, we have noted similarities with other countries moving towards greater democracy (Hatalak *et al.* 1998).

In more recent times, political changes have resulted in modern versions of colonialism. With the fall of communism and of apartheid in South Africa, western policing experts have been invited to advise governments in the new democracies on law enforcement and to help 'South Africa's police [change] from a paramilitary force into a community-friendly organisation' (J. Garland, *Scarman Centre News*, vol. 2, no. 2, June 1998). These developments have been described as part of the trend towards globalization, the spread of the same values and institutions to most of the nations of the world. Another partial version of this has been happening in Europe (Heidensohn 1997; Sheptycki 1998). In this case, the pressures have come through the political growth of the European Union where, although – in its earlier forms as the 'Common Market' and the 'Community' – there was little interest in criminal justice matters, that situation changed in the 1990s.

The first initiatives towards coordinating policing activities came from individual governments (Fijnaut 1991) and it was only with the 1991 Maastricht Treaty that justice and home affairs were formally included on the European agenda and then only at an intergovernmental level. Nevertheless, this and related changes have resulted in what some writers call 'transnational policing' in Europe (Sheptycki 1995a). It is clear that economic and political changes in Europe have resulted in some very distinctive developments and these in turn, have attracted considerable academic interest from researchers outlining and analyzing them (Benyon *et al.* 1993; Hebenton and Thomas 1995; and Anderson *et al.* 1995).

In introducing his text of selections on the comparative literature on policing, Mawby distinguishes approaches to the subject which fall 'into three groups...[of]...policing across a range of societies ...of..."transnational processes" and those that focus on particular issues in policing' (1999a, pp. 1–2). Our project can be placed in all three categories and while we acknowledge the worth of Mawby's taxonomy, we have followed a somewhat different path for our own analysis.

Putting women in the frame

First, we need to make several observations about much of this work. Unsurprisingly perhaps, most of the major studies published in this area have little to say about our main topic: 'any attempt to take an issue such as...the place of policewomen...would have been patchy, with data readily available in some countries and relatively sparse in others' (Mawby 1990, p. 192). More significantly, this gap has often been a matter of little concern to the authors. The considerable body of work on Anglo-American policing, for instance, largely ignored both the *distinctive* features of women's entry into law enforcement in both nations and the notable features they had in common (Heidensohn 1992). This marginalizing of women's contribution was, of course, also a feature of criminology until the late 1960s when feminist perspectives were first applied to the field (Heidensohn 1968; Smart 1977; Rafter and Heidensohn (ed.) 1995; Heidensohn 1996b). Since then, as well as having some impact on the subject, there has been a growing understanding of the importance of gender in relation to crime and criminal justice (Messerschmidt 1993, Newburn and Stanko (eds) 1994; Jefferson 1996).

There is a significant parallel in the case of police studies, but with an important exception. Police studies have, almost from their inception, focused on 'cop culture' and its features, as Reiner, for instance, stresses: 'The police world is one of "old fashioned machismo". Sexism in police culture is reinforced by discrimination in recruitment and promotion' (Reiner 1992, p. 124). Masculinity has thus always been an issue in research on the occupational culture of policing, either explicitly or implied. In the earliest attempts to define the 'working personality' of the police officer, Skolnick argued that 'the combination of danger and authority' plus the need to produce results were crucial (1966, p. 44). Considerable debate has flourished around the questions of what policing is, what factors produce police culture(s) and if and how they are linked (Reiner 1992; Rawlings 1995; Chan 1997). These themes are too large and complex to develop here (although we shall follow up aspects of them below). Some arguments are, however, crucial for our understanding of comparative analysis.

Broadly, much research has emphasized the unique trait of policing, namely force: 'police work consists of coping with problems in which force may have to be used' (Bittner 1990, p. 256). From this definition derives the image of the officer under threat 'behind every corner he (sic) turns or door-bell he rings, some danger, if not of firearms at least of fists' (Reiner 1992, p. 110). This perception can in turn lead to an 'elision which is frequently made: *coercion* requires *force* which *implies physique and* hence policing by *men*'

(Heidensohn 1992, p. 73) (original emphasis). Of course, part of this contention is empirically based, the majority of officers in most police forces *are* male. However, to argue from assumptions about the nature of policing that this must be so, is misleading; theoretically at least, it is possible to envisage law enforcement agencies with a majority of female staff (Young 1991; Brown 1997).

In exploring comparative approaches, we shall not keep repeating these caveats: this is not intended to be a critical review of their gender blindness (for such accounts, see Brown 1997 and Heidensohn 1998). Instead, we shall be trying to construct an analytical framework using the best and most promising parts.

Fixing frameworks

Attempts to classify law enforcement practices have quite a long history, although to do so for purposes of study is a more recent aim. Early in the twentieth century, Raymond Fosdick described 'English' and 'Continental' systems and stressed how different they were. In particular, he stressed that the 'English' form derived its power from a popular mandate, based on an ancient form of community constabulary, later rationalized into the 'new' police of London. He contrasts this with 'Continental' patterns where the power of autocratic states, such as Prussia from the eighteenth century, required the control of crime and disorder. He noted the quasi-military characteristics of the latter, their very wide range of powers from welfare administration to spying on the populace. (Fosdick 1915, cited in Mawby 1990). In fact, more than a century before Fosdick's own journeys to Europe and his (perhaps uncritical) accounts of his observations appeared, the 'Continental' model was recognized and described in Britain. At that period, however, this typification was invoked with scorn and as a challenge to successive attempts to introduce modern policing.

> Much of the resistance to the police legislation from 1785 to 1856 was couched in a rhetoric drawing on the supposed traditional liberties of Englishmen...a continuing strain of rhetoric [denounced] each step as a sinister French, Russian or Venetian (but at any rate distinctly continental) usurpation of the traditional English rights of self-government (Reiner 1992, pp. 16–22).

Historical accounts of the origins of the Metropolitan police in London are highly contested (see Reiner 1992 for an outline and an essay at synthesis). It is nevertheless clear that there were deliberate policies of differentiating the 'new' police from their European counterparts. They were, at first, a wholly uniformed force, their purpose was crime prevention, not the management of public order, they were deliberately non-military in uniform and were unarmed (Emsley 1997).

Several modern authors who have tried to develop taxonomies of police systems have followed Fosdick's lead and recognized the English/Continental divide. Bayley, the pioneer in this field, proposed a threefold typology which he described as 'authoritarian, oriental and Anglo Saxon' forms (1982). The first of these clearly has parallels with the continental form and is characterized as military, while the second, based on Bayley's own research on Japan, emphasizes close community ties. While Bayley's overall approach has been criticized by writers such as Brewer *et al.* (1996, p. 227) for rendering complex differences within agencies and nations in too facile a way, Mawby adapted aspects of Bayley's framework to classify early modern police systems to compare eight examples.[1] In this analysis, the only significant difference noted between England and Wales and the USA is the carrying of arms by the police in the latter. However, in a more recent review, he has argued that 'there are considerable differences between the British, US and Canadian police' (Mawby 1999c, p. 52). He comes to no final conclusion, but does question assumptions about the differences between 'so-called Anglo-American tradition and other police systems' (*op. cit.*). At the end of his earlier study, Mawby concludes that these categorizations do retain some value in the late twentieth century, although with modifications. He describes Hong Kong as still evidencing 'many of the characteristics of a colonial force... France and the USSR can still be identified with the continental model' (Mawby 1990, p. 198). Among his other examples, he found Japan, China and Cuba 'having police systems that might best be described as comprehensive or pervasive, distinguished from the colonial or continental models by their greater emphasis on welfare' (*op. cit.*, pp. 198–9). The situation in the Netherlands and Canada, he suggested 'is more ambiguous... Anglo Saxon policing traditions intermingle with influences from continental and colonial systems respectively' (1990, p. 199).

---

[1] Since the publication of this book, Hong Kong has returned to China and the Soviet Union has split into separate states.

These conclusions mirror much (although not all) of what a series of commentators on 'Anglo-American' policing have argued. They have noted the common historical heritage of the parish constable (Beckman 1980), the conscious learning from the Metropolitan police model, first in New York City and later elsewhere (Miller 1977). There have probably been more studies comparing policing in Britain and the USA and/or discussing whether there is indeed such a phenomenon as Anglo-American policing and how it may be changing (McKenzie and Gallagher 1989).

Less attention has been given to the question of whether this model can be found in various forms elsewhere. Explorations of colonial policing, most of which have focused on experiences in former British colonies, emphasize that in what might be termed 'New Commonwealth' countries, Britain introduced not the 'policing by consent' approach of the home country but the centralized, more militaristic system which had its prototype in Dublin, and later the Royal Irish Constabulary (Brogden 1987; Emsley 1997). Ahire in his account of the history of imperial policing in Nigeria points out that 'The RIC provided a model for colonial policing in general, and remained a tower of influence on the organization and development of the police in Nigeria in particular' and he cites Sir Charles Jeffries, a former senior civil servant in the Colonial Office who also concluded that 'the really effective influence on the development of colonial police forces during the nineteenth century was not that of the police of Great Britain, but that of the Royal Irish Constabulary' (Ahire 1991, p. 30). Ahire points out the parallels between Ireland and Nigeria under British rule 'the RIC was a paramilitary organisation . . . well trained in military drill and the use of firearms . . . It was conferred with immense powers . . . in place of the "rule of law"' (Ahire 1991, pp. 54–5).

Most of the research on this topic has considered former British colonies and has for instance explored 'imperial linkage' between the mother country and both states which were 'settled' and 'those' which were 'pacified' for trade purposes. Cole remarks in a review 'civilian policing structures were predominant in "settlement" colonies of North America, Canada and Australia, whilst para-military policing was common in "pacified" colonies located mainly in Africa, Asia, Central and South America' (Cole 1999, p. 89). Anderson and Killingray (1991, 1992) maintain that colonial policing has been as much influenced by events in the respective colonies as by the models from the imperial power. There has been increasing comment on colonial systems other than the British empire; Cole notes the similarities between France, Germany, Spain and Portugal in producing centrally controlled police forces, although he observes that the degree of para-militarism varied considerably. Shelley treats the situation in the states which were previously part of the Soviet Union as one in which the 'Soviet...model...was exported and imposed on diverse countries' (Shelley 1999).

Australia, New Zealand and to some extent Canada, were 'settler' states, since the occupying power, originally British, brought in a majority population which came eventually to dominate the indigeneous peoples. In these nations, the parallels and shared culture with British policing are notable (Finnane 1990) despite significant differences. In Queensland, for instance, Prenzler argues, 'The frontier situation...led to the adoption of a relatively intense organisation along the lines of the Irish Constabulary...The force had all the trappings of the military, and discipline was strictly hierarchical' (Prenzler 1997, p. 121). Indeed, this has continued into the late twentieth century with the formation of the Australian Federal Police based on advice from British sources, and a senior British officer being appointed as the Commissioner for New South Wales in 1996, following a series of scandals and concerns in that force.

Much comparative work focuses as we have already indicated on differences within versions of the British/American forms of policing. Yet it probably retains its value as an ideal typical model for use in analysis of this kind. Even in an article which is a sustained critique of this idea, Reiner paradoxically proves this point, while insisting 'that there is no single English model: the key features of English policing have varied considerably' (Reiner 1992, p. 16). He goes on to present a reasoned account of policing using the 'English model' as an heuristic device. His somewhat gloomy conclusions for 'post-modern times' are that 'the English model...will disintegrate', and something more like a continental form will develop (p. 41).

Fixing females in a framework

Despite such scepticism, we suggest that it is both helpful and instructive to look at the experiences of women in law enforcement around the world through a series of frames. The first of these we propose to call by the shorthand term of 'cops'. This is widely recognized as slang for police officers in England and Wales, the USA and Australia (although not, interestingly, in Ireland); it is also shorter and clearer than Anglo-American, Anglo-Saxon, Anglo-Celt and, we trust, less potentially offensive. For the second group of nations and systems we use the title 'gendarmes'. We apply this term mainly to continental and authoritarian systems which have military forms or origins. We differ from several other authors in retaining a category of colonial systems within our framework, but at the same time linking it to the other sections, notably of course, to the cops and the British traditions. We also add a further dimension of transitional states and note a dimension of transnationalism to take account of increasing globalization developments in Europe and of some of the complexities of the sharing of ideas and practices concerning women in policing.

A paradox confronts the researcher seeking information and illumination on the role of women in policing. On the one hand, as each of us has noted in separate reviews conducted nearly a decade apart, 'surveying the literature on women and policing in an international context, revealed a lack of material, or rather, a limited supply' (Heidensohn 1992, p. 106; Brown 1997, p. 12). On the other, Mawby, writing somewhat earlier, could claim that '*vis-à-vis* police-women . . . international comparisons are well-established' (Mawby 1990, p. 8). The clue to this seeming contradiction lies in the second part of the sentence just quoted where Mawby adds 'and indeed *historically based on the strategies of early reformers*' (*op. cit.*, emphasis added). It is indeed the case that, whereas for policing in general, the collection and analysis of comparative data emphasize the setting up and institutionalizing of law enforcement, often by many years, the introduction of women into policing was *preceded* by campaigns which were both local and specifically targeted and in turn linked to an international women police movement.

In Chapter 3, we discuss the entry of women into policing and the opposition which the pioneer policewomen encountered. As we note there, the movement was influenced by several factors, including both first wave feminism and moral reform groups. International links between predecessor organizations and earlier reformers existed prior to the forming of the women police movement. Indeed, urging the entry of women into policing was a regular feature of the agenda of many organizations with other broader aims in the late nineteenth century and early twentieth century. The International Bureau for the Suppression of the White Slave Trade (whose telegraphic address was 'Chivalry, South West London') sent a letter to the Home Secretary on 22 June 1914 about the resolution passed at their international congress held in July 1913 on the need for women police. (H.O.45.309485). Writing to the Home Secretary in the following year on the same topic, Margaret Damer Dawson quoted 'America and other countries where there was both discussion of and concern for the protection of women, and arguments for "a trained body of women" to fulfil that role were cited' (*ibid.*, 28 July 1915).

In March 1916, Damer Dawson and Mary Allen were at the Home Office to press their case, again using the examples of women police in the USA, the Netherlands and Denmark in support. Prenzler reports that in Queensland, the last Australian state to admit women into its police force, there was a powerful coalition voicing its support, with the Catholic Archbishop of Brisbane, a key figure, as well as women's suffrage groups, and 'comparisons were made repeatedly with Britain, the United States and the other Australian states' (Prenzler 1998, p. 122). Schulz, in writing of the history of women's role in policing in the US, notes the commitment, in name at least, of the pioneers to international links. The International Association of Policewomen was formed in 1915; despite its name Damer Dawson was the only non-North American member (Schulz 1995a, p. 44). Later in its history, a publication called *Policewoman's International Bulletin* was produced; among its editorials, it criticized British and European policewomen (*op. cit.*, p. 50). Schulz emphasizes the close ties of the early US female officers to social work, their stress on separation from male officers and their work and their disagreements with the British approach. Only in much more recent times has the IAP's successor body, the IAWP really taken on board an international perspective (Schulz 1998).

In part, this is obviously due to the fact that the USA is such a large and powerful nation that organizations within it do not necessarily need the support of wider links to achieve their aims. Nevertheless, as Schulz points out, the IAP leaders misread their situation and failed to see that they needed support from bodies other than their advocates in temperance and moral reform groups. 'Policewomen owed their existence to groups outside the police establishment. Their *ability to succeed was based on forces outside the police establishment*' (Schulz 1995a p. 55). Not realizing this as their true position, the IAP fell into decline, as did the role of women police in the US which was stagnant during the Depression.

Much the most fascinating example of the strategic use of international comparison to promote the role of women in policing was based partly on an illusion. From 1927 until 1937, The *Policewoman's Review* appeared regularly. It carried many accounts of women in law enforcement around the world: in Detroit (vol. II, no. 18, Oct. 1928), in Poland (Vol. VII, no. 11, 1934) and Brazil (vol. V, no. 4, Aug. 1931) as well as regular commentaries on the *International Committee for Women in Police* (vol. I, no. 1, May 1927). It is a valuable source in many ways; however, it is also misleading. 'Commandant' Mary Allen features frequently, often in photographs in which she is always in uniform; Allen had, of course, no longer any official claim to this title. Apart from her activities during the War, she had briefly been recalled to serve with the British occupying forces in Germany where she helped to set up the Women's Welfare Police in 1923. This unit was disbanded in 1925 and reorganized in 1926. In 1934, *The Policewoman's Review* (vol. VIII, no. 1, May) was celebrating Allen's role in this, and these congratulatory articles recur throughout the journal's life. Yet, as we recount in a later chapter, Allen and her partner Damer Dawson had been defeated in their aims for policewomen, and their organization, the Women's Auxiliary Service, played no further role in official policing. Yet Allen, who presumably financed the Review, maintained a successful impact, often leading others to believe that she was a senior police officer and maintaining and promoting the image of women police, especially abroad (Lock 1979; Carrier, 1988).

It was not only women in English-speaking countries who sought links with those from other nations to promote the cause of women police. As numerous entries in *The Policewoman's Review* show, support for the movement and some clear achievement of its purposes was widespread both before and after the First World War. This was always part of wider aims of social protection. The targets especially were young women and girls likely to be lured into, or already ensnared in, vice, and the maintenance of order in public places where women and children went were key common concerns. In European countries with continental police systems, police sisters or matrons were the first female entrants to the police. Here too, efforts were made to collect comparative data and establish links: as early as 1911, Beaujon undertook a systematic study of women's role in policing in German-speaking cities in Europe on behalf of a Dutch women's organization and presented the material to obtain her doctorate. What distinguishes the experiences of most European nations is the rise of facsim in the 1930s and the impact of the Second World War. Among the consequences of these changes were fundamental shifts of frontiers (several of the cities described by Beaujon as German in 1911 can no longer carry that title today) and the reformation of law enforcement and other major institutions.

In some cases, this has led to distinctive patterns of occupation or transfer. Twice in the twentieth century, women officers from Britain were sent to Germany to (re)form the women police there. More recently, former communist states have sought assistance in changing and training their law enforcement agencies in order to police the new democracies. In addition, developments in the European Union have meant that its member states, especially those party to the Schengen agreement on cross-border policing, have had to align aspects of policing. There are major and ongoing debates about many aspects of these trends and their impact on human rights and civil liberties (McLaughlin 1992; Sheptycki 1995a; and see Heidensohn 1997 for a review). An important step was taken in 1989 by a group of senior Dutch policewomen who, with the support of their government, held a conference which led directly to the setting up of the European Network of Policewomen. Its main objective is 'optimizing the position of policewomen in European police services' and its strategy is described as 'coordinating, motivating and advisory' (ENP 1998). To achieve these aims, it helps to form and support national networks of policewomen, carries out projects and research and provides conferences and training. So far, ENP is unique, although the Australasian women police have sought to emulate this approach.

Our short survey of international links and their role for women in policing illustrates that there are particular issues attached to comparisons of the female officers. Categories, such as those we propose to use, can be helpful in classifying systems and marking distinctions. However, in more than one sense, women's experience of law enforcement seems to have more in common, across agency and national boundaries, with their female colleagues than with those whom they work with everyday. This may in part be because, even before there were official policewomen in most countries, the pioneers of the movement sought to internationalize it as a key aspect of their entry strategy. It is interesting to note that the ENP, although it has a fundamentally different basis from the early international alliances, participated in the 1995 UN World Conference on Women, and as a result organized an international conference on the role of the police in combatting violence against women. To the outside observer, this appears to resemble the validating links between the pioneer policewomen and their outside advocates dedicated to feminist causes.

Comparative tool kits

One of us has already suggested elsewhere that three conditions need to be met in order to study crime comparatively. 'There must be sources of material and data with which to make comparisons . . . second, translatable concepts have to be available to make possible the collecting, ordering and analysis of such data. Finally, some kind of framework, part universe of discourse, part set of common concerns, must exist' (Heidensohn 1991, p. 10). Nelken has criticized this approach for being too positivistic and he is probably right (1994, p. 239). We have thus adopted a form of discourse analysis later in this book and in the present chapter focused on frameworks with a somewhat sceptical eye. In later chapters the respondents to our research recount how *they* perceive their roles, their work and their own agencies. In a later consideration of comparative research on criminal justice, Nelken distinguishes between three approaches which he describes as 'behavioural science . . . interpretivist . . . and legal comparativist' (1997, p. 561) and outlines some of the key problems with each of them. Once again, we find ourselves employing all of these approaches in this project, and as we show below, are conscious of the limitations of them all.

Nevertheless, we should say something here about comparative method and technique. Material on policing across the world varies enormously. The data recorded are usually less reliable for comparison than even recorded crime figures. For example, 'police' may mean very different things according to the place or time they are in. Many western countries have civilianized their police some years ago, leaving key tasks to sworn officers (Reiner 1997). This trend has not gone so far in former Communist States where armed officers may still administer the driving-licence system. For member states of the EU, Benyon and his colleagues have produced very useful summaries of key features of the enforcement agencies of each of them, including the numbers of women. In other countries a combination of local reports, produced as part of the requirements of accountability, and research studies are available. As far as possible, we have used English language sources, although some European countries publish summaries of key findings in English. Again, it is interesting to note that the ENP which compiles and collates data on policewomen has used English as its working language since its inception, even though its board members were mainly Dutch for its first five years.

Translatable concepts

Systems for classifying law enforcement organizations sit somewhat awkwardly around the phenomenon of women in policing. We have proposed adaptations and caveats and still believe the comparative task to be worth undertaking. Further, we want to point out a series of key concepts which have emerged solely in the literature on policewomen. Although they all derive from direct research contacts with female officers, they are from very varied sources and methodologies. Susan Martin was a participant observer in the Washington D.C. Police Department, as was Jennifer Hunt in 'Metro City'. John Brewer uses reports of an ethnographic study of the RUC in Belfast made by his research associate Kathleen Magee, while Jones, Heidensohn and Larnier all interviewed female officers in a variety of settings. All these authors propose concepts of how they perceive female officers manage their role and status.

Martin's is the first and classic version; she enrolled as a special-reserve officer and sought to find out how women adapt to a male occupational culture. Their adaptations form a continuum from 'defeminized' women at one extreme, who lose or mask their femininity and compete directly with males. At the other end are 'deprofessionalized' women who accept subordination, prefer indoor tasks to patrol and do not compete. Martin (1980) placed twenty-eight officers on a continuum from POLICEwomen to policeWOMEN to mirror these categories. Most (twenty-one) officers are somewhere in between and they are often clearly struggling to balance aspects of their roles. Jones, writing of the 'Medshire' force in Britain, distinguished a similar pair of responses of 'traditional' and 'modern' styles (1986).

Jennifer Hunt presents a more extreme and interesting version of strategies for coping with the cop culture of Metro City in the USA. She describes her own behaviour as a participant 'rebel' who was wilder, more aggressive with a 'combat personality' who would act crazy (1984, p.290). Her purpose was to create for herself a distinct identity which would overcome male resistance to female officers. She argues that she was really colluding with a masculine myth about the danger of policing. Police are only street sweepers, their manhood 'illusory', their tasks in practice: 'social relations, paper work, and housekeeping in the public domain' (1984, p. 294). In a reversal of the Martin and Jones concepts, Hunt is suggesting that 'feminine' women pose the most threat to their colleagues. She does suggest too, that some other female officers were also engaged, much as she was, in constructing new categories for themselves (1984, p. 293).

This approach is taken much further by Brewer who argues that, since policing is such a male domain, policewomen develop specially constructed identities as, in this case, Amazons or Hippolytes:

> the gender of policewomen in the work setting is a social construction that is interactionally accomplished in the job rather than being a simple reflection of their sex roles outside the workplace. The masculinity of some . . . and the femininity of others are resources used by policewomen in their different ways in order to function (Brewer 1991b, p. 244).

He stresses that these are conscious processes and that the women can be observed acting in quite different ways when not 'on the job'.

In a somewhat similar way, one of us found that both British and US female officers constructed their identities and strategies around a series of key concepts. They had varying degrees of control over their accomplishment of identity and career success; most of them sought, for instance, to use professionalism in order to impress male colleagues (Heidensohn 1992). In relation to the management of public order situations, women from both groups used similar tactics to those of their male colleagues; they differed from them in their considerable consciousness about how they presented themselves and dealt with their situations. They had 'developed ways to construct "presences" and demonstrate them in challenging situations' (Heidensohn 1994b, p. 300). Drawing on the work of John Brewer, and producing the most complex taxonomy so far, Mark

Lanier outlines a three-by-four table, derived from observing only twenty officers. His categories, he suggests, are evolutionary and are a mixture of strategic and descriptive. He does not seem to be clear on how chosen and constructed they are.

These approaches, unique to studies of women officers offer challenges to comparative study. All are based on research in the USA or the UK, with the exception of Heidensohn (1992, 1994b) and Brown (1997), none covers international comparison and most are very locally based. How applicable are they to other systems in other cultures? How valid are they still? Do they offer helpful insights into a range of aspects of women's role in policing or only to adaptations at street level to cop culture? We now turn to our analytical tasks to address these questions.

3

The Role of Women in Policing

Introduction

Commentators on policing have noted its particular association with men and male values (Toch 1976, p. 44; Heidensohn 1992, p. 202; Schulz 1995a, p. 7; Brown 1997, p. 13). It has been argued that policing is 'an almost pure form of hegemonic masculinity' (Fielding 1994, p. 47). Hegemonic masculinity is defined by Coyle and Morgan Sykes (1998, p. 264) as 'masculinities based on holding and preserving male power and privilege within society and subordinating groups outside the dominant class'. They argue that non-traditional women, and we extend this to include those who seek entry into domains that are solely male preserves, are threatening to men and in need of control by them. Coyle and Morgan Sykes show for example how early twentieth century opposition by men to women's suffrage was positioned in a discourse of patriotism in the United States, that is, to support women's campaign for the vote was un-American. In Britain, they suggest that 'medical evidence was garnered to construct women's social protest as a war against nature, with women being represented as rejecting men and constituting a third sex' (Coyle and Morgan-Sykes 1998, p. 266).

This chapter seeks to identify the discourses within which women's entry and progression within policing are located. We use methods from *Discourse Analysis* (Coyle 1995) to interpret both official and unofficial contemporary records. (See Appendix 1 for further details of this methodology.) Discourse Analysis is a method of inquiry that interrogates verbal or visual material in terms of its constructive properties as well as the function that the material serves. Functions can be justificatory, accusatory, blaming or questioning. Thus the analysis is about the construction of a

42

social reality, in this case by men of policewomen, and the functions this serves, to defeminize or deprofessionalize them. Discourse Analysis is thus not a portrayal of some objective truth: rather it seeks to comment on the constructive processes and their purposes. In this way we seek to add a dimension to histories of women police (Martin 1979; Heidensohn 1992; Schulz 1995a) and, more particularly, to extend Heidensohn's (1992) conclusions made with reference to an Anglo-American comparison.

Entry of women into policing

The early histories of women's entry into policing are located within the Anglo/American/Australian tradition and European models of police 'sisters'. The idea of 'women' police officers was simply not entertained until the middle of the nineteenth century. The first suggestions were couched in terms of this being a preposterous proposition. An early *Punch* cartoon of 1851 shows a tentative woman peeler's approach to a rather disreputable looking street hawker. Another cartoon in the *Illustrated London News* dated 1852 shows two types of women police officer facing an unruly mob: one attractive, the other brutish but both are ineffectual.

EFFICIENCY OF FEMALE POLICE IN WHAT IS VULGARLY CALLED A JOLLY ROW.

Source: Illustrated London News, 1852.

These early cartoons underpin the major objections to women as police officers that presaged the persistent resistance to their entry into policing. On the one hand women's frail physiques not only ill befit them to handle violent behaviour, thus deprofessionalizing them as police officers, but their sexual attractiveness may act as an incitement to more unruly behaviour. On the other hand, the possibility of being able to handle a mob could only be done by mannish women who, having physical prowess to do so, are defeminized, so disqualifying them as women. This use of imagery to deprofessionalize and/or to defeminize women police officers was not only to recur and prevail to the present day but also to occur in other policing traditions.

The closest women got to being police officers in the nineteenth and early twentieth centuries was through impersonation. Vesta Tilley, star of the British Musical Hall adopts a police uniform to sing 'A policeman's lot is not a happy one'. An early American silent film portrayed a woman who, as a joke on her boyfriend, dons his police uniform and comes to grief in various misadventures. It is with great relief that she changes her attire and returns the 'troublesome' uniform to its rightful owner (Schulz 1995a, p. 38).

In Australia, Tynan (1995) notes that prior to 1840 women who had emigrated as convicts were regarded almost uniformly as objects of sexual gratification – damned whores. By the middle part of the century the bourgeois family was being promoted as the most suitable form of social organization for the new country. Women were entrusted with the moral guardianship of the emerging nation's children and were expected to curb rebelliousness in young men, and install submission in young women preparatory to their roles as wives and mothers. The first-wave feminists in Australia, aligned with the Christian Temperance Union, fought for the introduction of women into the police as a source of moral influence – 'God's police'.

Origins of the idea of women in law enforcement had arisen in the United Kingdom as a consequence of the activities of philanthropists, moral rescue campaigners and the social hygiene movement of the late nineteenth and early twentieth centuries. Ryan, Ryan and Ward (1990) propose that these activities provided an outlet for women bored by their confinements, both literal and metaphoric, within the domestic sphere. One of the objects of their concerns was prostitution. In Britain, this was manifest by the movement for the repeal of the Contagious Diseases Act and the activities of the

National Vigilance Association (NVA). It was the use of male police to track female prostitutes that had prompted calls for women officers. Social purity connections also underpinned movements for the employment of women in policing in the United States (Heidensohn 1992) Europe (Levine 1994) and Australia (Prenzler 1994).

The first policewomen were employed on an experimental basis, in part to avoid embarassments caused by men's behaviour towards women suspects. Mitchell (1966, p. 211) writes that 'Germany was the first country to try and make use of women police – in 1905 – but the public reception of the *experiment* was so hostile that it had to be abandoned.' (Emphasis added.) In Scotland, the experiment was deemed more successful although the delays in dealing with the matter may yield some idea of the frustrations felt by those agitating for women police officers. In January 1914, the Glasgow Corporation agreed to receive a petition from the National Vigilance Association of Scotland requesting the employment of women to make inquiries into assaults against women. In March, the item was deferred pending a report by Baillie McMillan who was to visit Canada and the United States to assess how women were employed in this capacity there. The Corporation agreed to set up a subcommittee to consider the issue in the light of Baillie McMillan's assessment. This was duly considered in June 1915 when it was agreed that a female officer be appointed as an experiment for one year, she to have a salary of £2 per week. However, the Corporation felt they needed the sanction of the Secretary of State for Scotland. By September 1915, the Secretary of State indicated that his approval was not required whereupon Miss Emily Miller was duly appointed to look into criminal assaults on women and gathering of evidence for which it was difficult for men to collect. On October 10 1916, the Chief Constable submitted a letter to the Corporation indicating the success of the experiment and requesting that the appointment be made permanent. This was approved. (Minutes of the Corporation of Glasgow November 1913–November 1916.)

In Australia, women were employed as police officers in the first instance to prevent crime and engage in moral rescue rather than law enforcement. The justification was couched in terms of women being engaged in the control of women. Prenzler (1994, p. 259) observes: 'Legend has it that Inspector General Mitchell was influenced by the embarrassing spectacle of a policeman experiencing difficulties arresting several uncooperative women. Mitchell felt that women might be more effective arresting their own kind'. In 1915, two women, Lillian Armfield and Maude Rhodes, were appointed to the New South Wales Police to deal with truancy; patrol ports and railway stations to render assistance to young and women travellers not being met; to keep an eye on houses of ill-repute (*Daily Telegraph*, 26 June 1915).

Schulz (1995a, p. 7) traces the route taken by American women from volunteer Quakers – who sought to care for incarcerated female prisoners through the police matron movement – to the appointment of the policewomen. Schulz (1995b, p. 374) suggests that the appointment of Alice Stebbins Wells in 1910 as the first attested policewoman in the United States was seen as a continuation of the process of professionalization of women within the police environment overlapping the matron movement within correctional institutions. Thus, women police were recruited in the model of social workers, a point also made by Maniloff (1998, p. 3) with respect to the recruitment of early French policewomen.

The agitation for women's suffrage and the activities of the militant suffragettes represents another influential strand in the police women's movement. This consciousness and conscience of articulate middle and upper class women, about the plight of their less advantaged sisters, had been raised as a consequence of the former's clashes with the law as a result of civil disobedience in campaigning for the vote (Schulz 1995b, Tynan 1995, Weinberger 1995). There emerged a feminist agenda for reform which sought greater protection for women within criminal justice agencies (Radford 1989). Levine (1994, p. 41) suggests that there was a direct contradiction between the social purity motivations of some suffrage campaigners and those who espoused radical ideas about free love or the forging of passionate friendships between young, single, upper class women caught up in the excitement of political activism. This dichotomy reappears in slightly different guises throughout our analyses and underpins feminine and masculine values that inform priorities in policing and its styles.

However, the principal catalyst activating the need for women police was the First World War. Ryan, Ryan and Ward (1990) chart the unpaid activities of the NVA, patrolling railway stations and ports protecting women from the scourge of white slavery, to the formation of early policewomen patrols at the outbreak of the War. With labour shortages brought about by conscription, not only was there mass employment of women but women were unsupervised by brothers, fathers and husbands who were away fighting (Woodeson 1993). Women might not only sell sex but also give sexual favours away free. The moral panic this engendered mapped neatly onto the social purity motives of the volunteer patrols. The Voluntary Women Patrols (VWP) was launched by the National Union of Women Workers whose aim was unashamedly to restrain the behaviour of men and women who congregated in the neighbourhood of military camps (Radford 1989, p. 30). The following excerpt from a VWP notebook provides a graphic example of the volunteers' motivation:

> I do not feel that our patrolling in the park will do much good until we have authority to speak to people. They are so utterly unashamed and indifferent and merely walking to and fro leaves them unmoved. Though I fear in saying this I am showing myself faithless in the unseen spiritual influence in which our work is based (Georgina Crosfield, 11 June 1916, Leeds).

A second group were the Women Police Volunteers (WPV). Margaret Damer Dawson was a joint organizer and her objectives seem to derive from social purity motives as demonstrated by her involvement in the NVA. The other co-organizer was Nina Boyle, a former militant suffragette. Nina Boyle's motivation was more reform of the police culture, as well as bringing justice closer to all citizens, not just women. A similar position was expressed as an underpinning motivation in the United States by Owings (1925, p. ix):

> [Women's police] bureaus are acting as a socialising agency to the whole police force, resulting in a better and more intelligent attitude on the part of policemen towards men, women and children requiring their attention ... affects the attitudes of judges and prosecutors trained in the individualistic, unsocial theory of a legal system seldom taking into account the protection of women.

Yet, never far away were the objections that women lacked the physique for police work:

> the reason why the [British] movement for employing women police is so slow is the idea of what police work means ... The average man thinks of police work as confined to the detection of crime and the bringing of criminals to justice, with the additional work of regulating traffic and other kindred services. All this seems to require physical strength and courage above everything else and for that reason it

is unsuitable work for women (Cecil Chapman J.P reported in *The Policewomen's Review*, vol. 1, no. 2, June 1927).

The legitimation for objecting to women officers is clearly seen in the expression 'unsuitable work for women' and in its implied criticism of thus making them absent from their suitable work. M.Faralieq, a French police captain, interviewed by *The Policewomen's Review* (vol. 2 no. 14, June 1928) expresses these sentiments exactly:

> What would happen in Paris if we put women policemen in the street? There would collect a jeering crowd of hobbledehoys, girls, men, women and children round every unfortunate policewoman. Not it is not possible. It is utterly impossible in France. In France woman rules in one domain. She rules her husband (at home) her children her house. But there she ends.

In India, the notion of women police officers was thought to interfere with their mandatory role as home makers (Mahajan 1982). Examples from early attempts by African women to form a women's police corps were met with contempt and vilification of ugly man haters who would be unable to deal with criminals (Segrave 1995).

Given the panic over sexual behaviour of young women and soldiers, the pragmatic reality was that women be employed to guard a nation's morals. A justification was needed to reverse the previous opposition to women police. In Britain, this was found in terms of an antidote to 'khaki fever' described at the time as follows: 'When quite ordinary men donned khaki, they become, in the eyes of a number of foolish young women, objects to be pestered with attention very few of them desired' (Mitchell 1966, p. 212). Thus, women become the 'controllers' of other women's (sexual) conduct, protecting the hapless tommy, and happily maps onto the social purity genesis of Damer Dawson's position. This resonates with the Morals Police or 'police des moeurs' where women were attached to police in various European countries in order to deal with 'women who come into the hands of the police as moral delinquents' (*The Policewoman's Review*, vol. 1, no. 1, May 1927).

Nina Boyle's faction represented a more politicized agenda to draw attention to men's violence against women and a role for women in both change as well as protection (Radford 1989). This dichotomy resulted in a split between leading protagonists of the WPV. The crunch came in Grantham with the imposition of a curfew on women that Boyle claimed was a virtual reinstatement of the Contagious Diseases Act with which she disassociated herself. The Damer Dawson faction had no such compunction, seeing the issue as mainly to do with the standing of the embryonic women's police, and thus complied with the implementation of the curfew. Radford (1989) draws attention to the importance of this split in that here was an early example of a divergence of principle and pragmatics. This divergence appears cross-culturally and reappears at critical stages in the progression of women in policing.

The rationale for developing policewomen's departments in the United States follows a similar pattern but with some variations. Schulz (1995b, p. 373) discusses the role of the charitable works which brought middle-class women into contact with poor women. She argues 'at the end of the Civil War another generation of women expanded this particular philosophy of "women's sphere" taking it far beyond jail and prison walls into other public sector areas.' Schulz (1995a) shows how there were two movements supporting the developments of police matrons and policewomen and how both were inextricably intertwined with social purity and early female reform traditions. The prevention and protection theories that underpinned the role of these early American policewomen located them firmly within the social worker ambit. Indeed, Schulz (1995b, p. 375) notes that some were called 'city mothers' and intervened in families whose lifestyles they believed required an injection of discipline. But Damer Dawson saw policing as a public service 'which as a matter of principle should involve women' (Radford 1989, p. 28). Schulz (1995a, p. 4) proposes that the early American policewomen did not see themselves as female versions of policemen and eschewed the notion of being 'little men', trying rather to separate themselves physically and functionally. Unlike the British policewomen at this time, the American women police 'were vehemently opposed to uniforms' (Schulz 1995b, p. 375). Early women police in Europe, such as Holland and Sweden, represented a middle position: they saw the need for a distinctive garb but wore nurses, uniforms and were identified as police 'sisters'. Swedish police sisters were concerned to influence vagrant women in order that they might take up some honourable means of livelihood, or to find homes for girls brought into conflict with the law so that they 'could straighten lives which have gone awry before it is too late' (*The Policewoman's Review*, vol. 7, no. 1, May 1933). This softer image may have muted the hostility of policemen which did not seem as extreme as that evident in Britain, Australia and the United States.

Another important development in the United States was the formation of the International Association of Policewomen in 1915 to advance the appointment and training of and support for women officers. This was eventually to disappear by the 1930s and was not to be reinvented until 1956. There was no equivalent European Association; rather, there appears to have been an energetic self promotion of the British model of women police by Margaret Damer Dawson and her deputy, Mary Allen. In 1920, Margaret Damer Dawson died and Mary Allen took over the leadership of the Women's Police Service (WPS). *The Policewoman's Review* provides a fascinating account of Mary Allen's self-promotional journeys around Europe to encourage the activities of nascent women police organizations in France, Spain, Scandinavia, Poland and Germany. Levine (1994, p. 67) notes that the British example served as a model for the development of women police bureaus in Canada, New Zealand, South Africa, and Australia. However, in 1926, the International Committee for Women's Police was established in Paris (*The Policewomen's Review*, vol. 1, no. 1, May 1927). Its aims were to: ensure women police have the full status and powers of their male colleagues; condemn the use of women in the *police des moeurs* or as *agents provocateurs* in the regulation of prostitution; and promote the right of women police officers to wear uniform. The role that this organization might have played in the development of women's police is not only unclear but seems to have been ignored in the official records and remains invisible to analysts of the history of policewomen. The modern reincarnation, European Network of Policewomen, was not to be formed until the 1990s believing itself to be the first international alliance of European policewomen.

We can now add to the conclusions about the origins of women's entry into policing drawn by Heidensohn (1992, p. 52):

● Heidensohn notes the opposition to the entry of women into policing in Britain and America. We find evidence that this was also the case in Australia and Europe. Our present analysis outlines the motives undermining women's policing aspirations: the need to protect the good woman (paternalistic concerns) from a job that was inherently unsuitable and to exclude women having a role in social control (patriarchal preservation). The discourses adopted for such arguments were notions of the 'unnatural' proposition in the accepted scheme of gender role and power relations (defeminization) and the 'unsuitability' of women as police officers (deprofessionalization). The rhetoric adopted to justify the incorporation of women into the police was as guardian of the nation's morals in order to *protect men*. Levine (1994, p. 72) argues that the transformation in accepting the idea of women police was very costly. She proposes that this resulted in a blurring of gender identity which was countered by extreme forms of masculinity demanded of men, ideas of vanquishment, conquest and aggression exaggerated by the First World War. This created a kind of vicious cycle in which the masculine basis of policing resisted the feminine encroachment even harder. Women officers were caricatured as masculinized or dismissed on the grounds of ineffectual femininity.

• Heidensohn also concludes in her Anglo-American comparison that early work of policewomen was directed into specialist roles. We note that this developed from the protectionist moral welfare claim calling for the employment of women within law enforcement. In the United States in particular, this characterized women police as social workers, a label that remained with them until the mid-1960s. *The Policewoman's Review* suggests that women's entry into policing in Sweden, Norway, Poland and France followed a similar pattern. We would add that consciousness raised as the result of political agitation and activist suffrage campaigns saw articulate, educated women in the courts and given custodial sentences that exposed them to the plight of women as offenders and victims of male violence. This led to a reformist agenda in which women were to play a role in changing policing. The legacy of these activities confirmed male notions of women's moral superiority in not only managing men's libidinous sexual conduct but also purifying the male police force (Ryan, Ryan and Ward 1990; Tynan 1995) and continued to dog debates about extending the numbers and role of policewomen.

• A further conclusion by Heidensohn of this early period was the notion of proselytizing by the pioneer policewomen in the United States and Britain. This was also found to occur in Australia and Europe with a number of the early women police officers achieving a certain amount of celebrity status, if not notoriety. We would extent this conclusion by pointing out that pioneer policewomen bore the brunt of ribaldry which fuelled the claims of detractors that policing was both unnatural and unsuitable as a job for women. The police women's movement in Britain was decried as 'a farcical manifestation of feminist agitation' (origin of this quotation is unknown but was cited in *The Policewoman's Review* (vol. 5, no. 2, 1931). Policewomen continually had to demonstrate their worth throughout 1914–18 by their 'good character and wealth of service [such that] the mouths of detractors may be closed' (Carden n.d.). Schulz (1995a, p. 24) describes the rather unflattering contemporary description of America's first policewoman, Alice Stebbins Wells, as 'a bony muscular person, grasping a revolver, dressed in anything but feminine apparel, hair drawn tightly into a hard little knot at the back [with] huge unbecoming spectacles'. A further extension to Heidensohn's conclusion about proselytizing is that the campaigning activities of Alice Stebbins Wells, Mary Allen and other early pioneers represents an early example of globalization. There is evidence that officials visited the United States and Britain to examine the experiment of women as detectives and police officers, and their assessments influenced the developments in women police in their respective home countries. Practice in Britain was exported to embryonic women's police departments in Germany, Poland and other European countries.

• Heidensohn noted the involvement of women police in controlling other women. We now can contribute further notions to this analysis. Firstly, women were seen as protectors of men from the unwanted attention of girls afflicted by 'khaki fever.' Secondly, there was not unanimity between the early women police pioneers. In England, there was a split in the leadership of the women's police movement with the apparently more co-operative, conformist Damer Dawson being able to persuade the members of the WPV to displace Nina Boyle's feminist ideals. Levine (1994, p. 55) suggests this represents a 'de-radicalization' in so far as policewomen's ambitions were only realizable by having them articulated within a framework of their specialized feminine attributes but in such a way that distanced them from their identification with other women. There was an inherent contradiction in women submitting to male authority in terms of their policing duties supervising wayward women, and the facts of their own lives which often drew them away from their duties as daughters or wives.

- An additional conclusion we can now offer are differences in attitudes of the early police women towards uniform. The American women officers were very clear in their sense of separation and had no desire to adopt a uniform. In Britain and Europe, there was a clear aspiration to be part of a uniformed service, although in Europe, this tended to be as police sisters in nurses' uniforms rather than the British desire to be uniformed police officers.

- Finally, there are differences in the rationales offered in the employment of the first policewomen. As well as the more obvious pragmatic concerns over manpower shortages and sexual licence as a consequence of the First World War, in the United States, the employment of female police officers was part of the process of professionalization of women's roles as criminal justice practitioners. In Britain, these first steps were seen as more tentative and experimental, whilst in Australia, the inspector general was influenced by developments overseas and the avoidance of potential embarrassment over policemen's inappropriate handling of women suspected of prostitution.

Restricted duties

In the aftermath of the First World War, Schulz (1995a, p. 31) quotes from an editorial in the journal *Woman Citizen* of March 1920 that policewomen were no longer an experiment but a fixture crying out to be taken seriously. In Britain, the Metropolitan Police announced that they accepted the principle of women police officers but decided to recruit not from Damer Dawson/Allen's WPS but the National Union of Women Workers' VWP. There are a number of reasons suggested for this. Ryan, Ryan and Ward (1990) argue that the VWP were more accommodating and co-operative than the WPS. Lock (1979) suggests that there had been some legacy of Nina Boyle's more radical thinking that had influenced the WPS in terms of their attitudes towards prostitution. Radford (1989) proposes that the explanation lay in anti-lesbianism. Doan (1997, personal communication) goes even further and suggests an anti-lesbian conspiracy. She argues that two law suits, one involving the dancer Maud Allen and another the writer Radclyffe Hall, had invoked a vigorous debate about 'the cult of the clitoris' said to have emerged through the exigences of women's involvement in

War work. Doan argues that lesbianism presented a threat to masculine hegemony especially within the realm of policing. Since criticism of the WPS leaders were made in terms of their styles of dress and other than 'normal' behaviour as women, Doan believes there is plausible evidence that the police were covertly involved in attempts to criminalize same sex relationships amongst women in the provisions of the Criminal Law Amendment Bill of 1921. Macready, the Metropolitan Police Commissioner had stated that he did not want 'vinegary spinsters' or 'blighted middle aged fanatics' (codes for lesbians) within the ranks of the post-war women's police (Levine 1994). Thus Radford (1989, p. 39) concludes:

> it should not be surprising that it was from the largely upper/middle class VWP that the Metropolitan Police recruited...when it finally accepted the need for policewomen in 1918. This organization had kept a much lower profile, content to operate within male definitions of the problem of prostitution and serve under male authority.

In England, women police officers were were still thought of as experimental. Sir Leonard Dunning (His Majesty's Chief Inspector of Constabulary for England and Wales) wrote in his annual report:

> I am not much discouraged by the fact that the experiment of employing policewomen has failed in some places, because it seems likely that in some instances the failure has been due to injudicious selection, in others want of imagination in their employment and in others to prejudice, especially where police administration is guided by too much tradition...The advocates for the employment of policewomen would probably be more successful if they tried to show that the efficiency of the police service would be improved rather than that the interests of one sex would be better served (HMIC 1923, p. 6).

The message is clear: if progress was to be made and the experiment deemed a success, women were to be quiet and acquiescent. Weinberger (1995, p. 102) describes this as innovation but in a staunchly conservative mode. Whilst the Metropolitan Police and the Inspectorate of Constabulary might have accepted the principle of women police, the staff association, the Police Federation, had not and regurgitated the objections to women officers:

> The [Constables] committee is unanimously of the opinion that the utility of women from a police point of view is negligible and does not justify the expenditure involved...with all the good will in the world and from a wholly impartial and disinterested starting point, we have been entirely unable to discern any

grounds warranting the formation of a force of women police... Police work is essentially a duty for which women are neither physically nor temperamentally adapted to perform successfully. Police work is men's work – a woman if there be one would be an unnatural product... Temperamentally, emotionally and physically women are fundamentally different from men, and if there is any work which demands personal characteristics quite the opposite of those which naturally distinguish women. That work is police work (Police Federation of England and Wales 1924, p. 10. Report of the Constables Committee).

The Scottish Police Federation expressed similar views 'It is not that the Scottish police are antagonistic to the employment of women, but any thinking man who knows anything about police work does not want to see a woman touching it at all. It is not a thing for women' (Kenna and Sutherland 1998, p. 70). The language used is striking, emphasizing men's entirely rational and reasoned arguments contrasting with women's emotionality and the 'unnaturalness' of policewomen, implying there are other duties for which they are naturally suited. Sir Leonard Dunning was willing to entertain the idea of women police in England and Wales but within strict limits:

Women in the police presents itself to many people merely as part of the feminist question. The first duty of the police is to prevent crime; they can do so by force, or by persuasion and advice... Force is better left to the man and so is persuasion when the person to be persuaded is male, but persuasion and advice offered to a female comes better from a female... Though the law lays blame on the male, the female may be strengthened in her resistance to male temptation or be dissuaded from being herself the temptress. Policewomen of the right sort can establish an influence in the streets and places of public resort which may do much to save girls from taking a step which cannot be retraced (HMIC 1925, p. 5).

The language here looks very much like the seductress and mother stereotypes employed by Kanter (1977) to describe women in business organizations. The rhetoric is either of the woman waiting to ensnare hapless men or her supposed moral superiority to protect the young and wayward. It is to be the right sort of 'good' policewoman extolling virtue which acts as a model to inhibit the immoral conduct of the wrong sort of girl. Indeed, advent of the woman detective was thought to have an enlightening effect on the criminal classes. K.R.G. Browne wrote in the *London Evening News* (and quoted in *The Policewoman's Review*, vol. 4, no. 39, July 1930):

A law breaker in danger of arrest thinks nothing of dotting male detectives on the conk or boko; what else... can one do to large, red-faced men in bowler hats. But the most desperate thug who ever robbed his grandmother of her old age pension would probably be willing to call it a day and go quietly if he were confronted by a really fair cop in a maiden's-blush chiffon and a hat from the Rue de la Paix.

The paradox of a young (and innocent) woman detective set against a desperado is striking, but the writer warns of the dangers that might befall the lady detective if the miscreant is her soul-mate. 'Torn between Love and Duty, how will she act? Will she bite the bullet and reach for the handcuffs, with a low choking sob? Or will she throw honour to the winds and urge her surprised but gratified prisoner to beat it?'

The lady detective presented other dangers to the conduct of policing. This was manifest in satirical pieces such as 'Eve goes sleuthing' (*Police Review*, 29 September 1933). The anonymous author writes 'The year 1933 will go down in police history as the year when the all-conquering modern female achieved her final conquest by being officially admitted into the mystic rites of criminal investigation.' The connotations attached to Eve are obvious and the writer leaves us in little doubt that the work of the detective will be compromised by the sweet young woman detective who 'is flirting brazenly with P.C. 49'. Possibly even worse is the prospect that wives, sisters and daughters may become detectives, restricting men to being mere uniformed beat sloggers; or unbearably, 'they may become detective inspectors and order us about – so that being on duty will be just like being at home'. If she is not actively flirting with the criminal, the policewoman becomes a spoiler of men's behaviour (a theme picked up by Susan Martin in her work on American policewomen some fifty years later which shows part of policemen's opposition to women is their potential for exposing men's sexual infidelities and use of raunchy language: Martin 1989a).

Caricatures of policewomen also appeared in the United States at this time (Schulz 1995a, p. 26). Women officers were represented as Amazons crowned with the old-time helmet and brandishing a club. They were seen as jokes appropriate for comic books and humorous periodicals. *Punch* in 1933 (16 October) carried a cartoon in which two male smash-and-grab robbers are making off with fur coats watched by a smiling, on looking policewoman with the caption 'and whatever will you rascals be up to next, eh?' To retain some femininity was to risk being viewed as ineffectual. To have the necessary prowess to equip her for the task challenged the policewoman's claim to femininity. Tynan (1995, p. 19) argues that this dilemma was also evident in Australia: 'On the one hand was society's hopes and expectations of what qualities women could bring to policing from their higher morality. On the other was what would bring the women police the respect and credibility they needed from their colleagues and superior officers.'

Weinberger (1995) argues that women were still expected to provide supportive roles extended from the domestic sphere as policewomen doing work that related to women and children. Not only this, but policemen's wives were still expected to provide unpaid administrative work and support to their police officer husbands. Weinberger (1995, p. 90) holds that 'in this way the main bastion of police masculinity remained unsullied and unbreached.' It was the long established practice of calling upon police wives to act as unofficial escorts, interviewers and minders of lost children that inhibited the development of policewomen's role and numbers. Weinberger's analysis suggested that by the 1930s the high rate of unemployment, combined with a loss of momentum of feminist consciousness, women police officers were no longer women with a mission but simply women with a desire to get away from home and the boredom of provincial life. They were caught between the progressive achievements of the pioneers and the inhibitory forces of male unemployment. Tynan (1995, p. 21) draws a similar conclusion for Australian women police during this period where a combination of high unemployment, a preference for hiring male breadwinners and a failure of feminist campaigners to sustain political pressure led to little growth in numbers of women in Australian police forces. Schulz (1995a, p. 80) proposes that in the United States too, there was a loss of public interest in feminism and reform activities associated with the progressive period. The Depression reinforced traditional gender demarcations such that there was active discrimination against women's employment.

The introduction of the Children's and Young Person's Act in 1933 in Britain increased policewomen's specialist work, and Weinburger (1995, p. 99) argues that they enjoyed their minority status and the public's attention for the work that they undertook. They felt cosseted, protected and privileged in the absence of street supervision. By being confined to domesticated roles and having a marginalized and subordinate status, they muted the hostility of male colleagues. Thus policewoman as temptress was transformed into suitable marriage partner. A cartoon of 1939 (*Police Review*, 6

October) shows a disapproving male sergeant watching a police-woman arm in arm with a male constable and being told 'You see, sir, they are getting married to-morrow.' Twenty years later (14 January 1959) *Punch*'s update of this sentiment shows a woman officer marrying a sergeant and using handcuffs instead of wedding ring to seal the event. Twenty years further on, *Police* (October 1977) was still carrying cartoons showing policewomen with their minds on marriage (and presumably not on their duty). These discourses are employed to convey images of policewomen as feminized but unprofessional, being compromised by their emotions and distracted by thoughts of marriage.

Yet, this is not the complete story. As is often the case with the histories of policewomen, there was a more upbeat presentation by women themselves. The WPS was staging photographs of heroic women on motorcycles or arresting suspects in the period after the First World War. *The Policewoman's Review* was presenting pictures of policewomen as women of action. The front cover of January 1934 (vol. 7, no. 9) saw a close-up of a young woman officer bestride a speeding motorcycle. *The Policewoman's Review* regularly had articles showing the varied activities of women officers in Europe and the Dominions. In its issue in 1931 (vol. 5, no. 3) Mrs Ulysses G. McQueen was featured as the first air policewoman serving in Beverly Hills California where she held the title 'aerial police investigator'.

In the United States, there is some evidence of the splits that had characterized the early development of women police in England. Gornall (1972) comments that in New York there was rivalry between the movement for police matrons and women police officers until these two groups merged in 1937. Schulz (1995b, p. 377) indicates that by the 1940s the image of policemen as crime fighter was emerging and was diametrically opposed to policewomen as social worker. Moreover, it was rare for municipal government officials or police chiefs to think of hiring women. Rather, demand came from outside bodies.

This was also true in England. Tancred (1941) notes the operation of the discretionary principle in the appointment of women officers in England and Wales whereby chief constables exercised what the Archbishop of York labelled 'Victorian prejudices' in resisting the hiring of policewomen. By 1940, the *Police Journal* (vol. 13, p. 330) was reporting that the Chief Constables of England and Wales were against the employment of women on the following grounds:

- that police work is done successfully without women
- their frail physique and the fact of their sex itself severely limits the use of women officers
- disputed claim of the advantages of women dealing with women (after all, women patients stubbornly cling to the ministrations of male doctors)
- it is useless to expect a hardened female offender to talk to a policewoman as there is a psychological barrier between the fallen woman and the good woman which effectively prevents communication
- women police contribute to their own unpopularity by not being able to take criticism or correction.

Once again the logic of the incompatibilities between the good and the bad woman are invoked in which (sexual) knowledge disqualifies women from being effective police officers, although clearly not doing so for men. Women in the United States seemed to fare little better. Schulz (1995a, p. 85) notes the dawn of the progressive era in American policing with the work of O.W. Wilson who was the architect of modern management principles being introduced into policing. However, he was not persuaded that women could take a leadership role in the new professionalism because of their 'tendency towards emotional instability which women display when under constant pressure'.

The views expressed by the Chief Inspector of Constabulary in Scotland were more positive. 'I am strongly of the opinion that the employment of further policewomen in the cities, large burghs, industrialised areas and garrison areas should be considered...the more one gets to know of policewomen's work the more one appreciates their helpfulness, kindness and acts of humanity' (Annual Report 1940, p. 6). Weinberger (1995) suggests that World War II brought surprisingly few changes to the role and status of policewomen. There was even a return to the earlier divisiveness. A Women Auxiliary Police Corps (WAPC) was formed, the officers undertook driving and clerical duties and were rather despised and resented by the members of the regular force. This was because some forces took on WAPC members instead of women police, so undermining the cause (Lock, personal communication 1998). Chief constables were still unwilling to appoint women officers. A *Police Review* article for 1939 (22 September) notes the reasons given by the Chief Constable of Hull:

It would not be safe for women Police in a blackout. It was customary in Hull to have Police patrolling in pairs in certain parts of the town, and it was necessary in certain instances to resort to force. While the activities of women social workers were accepted in good spirit, it would be a *dangerous incitement* to have Police-women in uniform. [emphasis added]

At the same time, women were being accused of 'causing' problems: by virtue of their gender, the Metropolitan Police were employing 'decoy doras' to combat soliciting. The *Montreal Daily Star* of 8 October 1940 reported that vice dens are to be cleaned up and soldiers and munitions workers protected by the deployment of girl detectives who will wear smart tailor-made suits, silk stockings and high-heeled shoes. Here is a beautiful example of the paradox facing policewomen: the good (police) woman should not have knowledge of explicit sexual behaviour yet she is called up to act the part of a prostitute. To do her job well as a police officer, she enters the domain of the fallen woman and so forfeits her position as a good woman. To do the job badly, based on ignorance of how prostitutes behave, and retaining the moral high ground, risks the charge of being labelled a poor police officer.

The policewoman still preserved her First World War role as antidote to khaki fever with the justification invoked in very similar language as twenty-five years previously. The rhetoric is that it is wayward girls who require control. The Archbishop of York wrote in 1943:

Around military establishments there often collect a number of silly girls who are a nuisance to soldiers and who occasionally through sheer foolishness run into moral danger. Male police, military or civilian, find it extra-ordinarily difficult to deal with girls of this type. Policewomen have the training and authority to deal with this class of girl (Women in Council Newsletter 32, January).

The American version of this is noted by Schulz (1995a, p. 104) who reports the activities of the 'victory girls' whose intentions towards soldiers in New York alarmed the authorities. Women officers reprised their First World War social protection role and were placed on patrol in Times Square.

But again, there appears an apparent contradiction in the deploy-ment of women officers. Women were used in dangerous undercover work and this illustrated the ambivalence of the police towards their women officers. *The Times* (1 January 1940) notes: 'The cunning which characterised the campaign of violence of members of the illegal

IRA led the Authorities to employ women police officers, several of whom were able to shadow Irish suspects without themselves being noticed. When they gave evidence in courts their names were carefully suppressed.' Cherrett (1990, p. 140) notes the irony for women in the New Zealand police during World War II who, largely protected from arduous duties, 'were sometimes expected to participate in demanding and dangerous undercover assignments'. This included infiltrating illegal drinking dens. The policewomen were instructed to allow themselves to be picked up by American servicemen and taken to night clubs where alcohol was being sold illegally.

The Second World War did not create new roles for American policewomen; rather, women were hired for their traditional police gender-specific functions (Schulz 1995b). It was to be the post-war years that witnessed a diversification of women's assignments in the United States of America. Women began to be teamed more with male officers and work on undercover assignments. They now routinely wore uniform and were armed. Schulz (1995b) also notes that during the 1950s, a different type of women was being brought into the police. Rather than the upper-class social worker, these new recruits were former military, middle-class careerists. Their career aspirations mirrored those of men. Women's self-image in society was changing. In 1956, the International Association of Policewomen relaunched itself as the International Association of Women Police (IAWP). In 1961, two New York women officers sued the police for not permitting them to take promotion examinations. Yet there was still underlying resistance. A Police Foundation symposium in 1974 noted the underlying resistance to policewomen based on: stereotyping (beliefs about physical inferiority and psychological instability); threats to the image of a gun-toting man of action; threats to family life through sexual liaisons between policemen and policewomen.

In England and Wales the official rhetoric was finally softening. By 1950, HMIC was reporting:

> Where supervision of the work of the growing numbers of policewomen is combined with a realisation by senior police officers that women, if trained and experienced in general police duties, will become even more skilful and experienced in the specialised forms of investigation, preventative work and protection of women and girls, then the value of policewomen to the community is constantly improved and extended. The fact remains that there are still some forces in which this value of the professional policewoman is not yet fully recognised (Annual Report, p. 8).

In 1947, the New South Wales Police Commissioner had toured overseas and observed the roles played by women internationally. On his return, he sought women volunteers to become involved in traffic duties. By the 1960s, women in New South Wales were employed in crime prevention and in 1971, women qualified as detectives for the first time (Tynan 1995).

By the 1960s, there was a shortage of women officers that actually worried the Metropolitan Police who began a recruitment campaign. Interestingly, the largest number of enquiries (32/119) came as a result of an advertisement in the *Lady*, a middle-class magazine. (PRO/HO 8590). Miss Barker, who was the senior woman officer from 1961 to 1966, indicated that the conception of women officers had changed. In former days, she claimed, they had been selected for their toughness and ability to undertake a man's job. Now the need was to do a woman's work requiring the officer to be feminine. Miss Barker wrote: 'success [in such recruitment] will mean marriage rates will be high particularly as they train and work with male colleagues. I would consider any move towards selecting a manly type of woman to undertake women's police work in the hope of retaining her services as definitely retrograde' (PRO/HO 8881). So women had not only officially been rehabilitated as feminine but as Metropolitan Commissioner Sir Robert Mark wrote in his autobiography:

I had always recognised that women were biologically necessary for the continuance of the force and were better able to persuade the public of our virtues as a service. In Leicester I had boldly ignored all the various Home Office exhortations and equipped them with court shoes, short skirts, air hostess tunics and shoulder bags. The effect was electric – our recruitment rocketed. So alas did our matrimonial wastage rates (quoted in Brown and Heidensohn 1996).

The sexual availability took a rather cruder form in the unofficial discourse. In 1971, *Police Review* carried a cartoon with a pneumatically busted woman officer being viewed by two overweight policewomen commenting on her ineffectualness with the observation 'Yeah Doris, I bet she couldn't stop a punch-up with a "Nah then, Nah then, What's it all abaht".' Another cartoon in the same year shows a woman police officer (Miss Lush) with an hour-glass figure standing alongside a knowingly expectant male constable with a sergeant exclaiming 'Whilst Opkins and I are searching around the lake, you and Miss Lush can be carrying on

'Yeah Doris, I bet she couldn't stop a punch-up with a "Nah then, Nah then. What's it all abaht."'

Source: *Police Review*, 2 July 1971.

over there in the hayfield.' Seven years on and the lascivious look on the face of two policemen becomes more explicit as they sit in their car watching a young and attractive policewoman wearing a short skirt with a frill of petticoat showing, to the caption 'I see the Federation wants shorter shifts for policewomen' (*Police*, October 1968). The sexual wiles of the women police were not just directed at their police officer colleagues. Rather than the villain being overcome by the innocent young lady detective of the 1930s, the policewoman is portrayed as using her sexuality more explicitly and expertly. A cartoon appeared in an Irish newspaper showing two sweating Gardai with coshes in their hands looking at an attractive policewoman sitting on the knee of an unshaven, battered villain, stroking his chin, saying 'Never mind the brutes, Spike. Just tell your darling little Doreen where it was you hid the swag (O'Kelly 1959, p. 75). This represents a loss of innocence with policewomen seen as having and using sexual knowledge. In May 1971, a rather different 'Doreen' makes her first appearance in the Police Federation's magazine *Police*. She is an overweight, large-breasted

Policewoman in Action :
*" Never mind the brutes. Spike.
Just tell your darling little Doreen
where it was you hid the swag."*
— Dublin Opinion

Source: Dennis O'Kelly (1959) *Salute to the Gardai 1922–1958* (Dublin Pareside Press).

policewoman whose contribution to a Federation conference, illustrated by three men making for the exit amidst smoke, is marked with the caption 'setting fire to your bra was hardly the way to get a motion through Conference Doreen!.'

Policewoman as an object of sexual interest is made very explicit. Women are represented to conform to male fantasies of desirable women, (i.e. feminized) and axiomatically ineffective police officers. However, they are also seen as getting an admission (professionalized) but doing so unfairly by using their sexuality to trap male suspects where their male colleagues have failed, and are thereby, deprofessionalized. But at the same time, the unattractive emasculating Doreen appears, suggesting that handling police tasks physically must disqualify you as a woman (that is defeminization): sentiments harking back to the *Illustrated London News* cartoon of 1852.

In commenting on the discourse constructing the policewoman's identity during this period, we see a consolidation of her presence in the police which itself is no longer disputed, but extension to her role, especially in investigative duties, is hotly contested:

- During the years between the World Wars, described as a latency period in which the energy of feminism fuelled by the suffrage campaigns had been exhausted, there was some consolidation. Policewomen's departments grew, albeit very slowly, in terms of numbers but the work revolved around women and children within a domesticated specialism. Recognition for undertaking 'women's work' brought with it affirmation from policemen and admiration from the public. Attempts to venture beyond the preserve of the policewomen's department resulted in the construction of the dangerous woman 'Eve' and the emasculating 'Doreen' who between them would undermine men's control over policing management and functions. Respect was bought at the price of unequal status and absence of sexual harassment (Weinberger 1995, p. 99).
- Promotion of women's entry into the police, their continuance and the extension of their roles were both facilitated and inhibited by men. A male view persisted that policing was an unsuitable job for a woman. However, men did play a key role in advancing the progress of women police. Whilst women had been used as typists in 1914 by the Prefet de police in Paris, it was a later Prefet, Roger Langeron, who decided in 1935 to use women operationally to assist in the city's juvenile bureau (Dene 1992). The Marques de Fronda conceived the idea of creating a nucleus of women officers in the Vigilance Department of the Spanish Police in anticipation of the problems arising from the International Exhibition of Barcelona in 1929 (*The Policewoman's Review*, vol. 4, no. 41, September 1930). Persuaded by the effectiveness of particular policewomen, the Commissioner for South Australia and later the Commissioner for Melbourne made public pronouncement of support thereby officially sanctioning their usefulness. This pattern was to repeat itself in Australia with Queensland Commissioner Ray Whitrod relaxing quotas on female entry in order to 'procure intelligence in policing – a quality in small supply when I began as Commissioner in 1971' (Wimshurst 1995, p. 287). Equally when his successor reintroduced the quotas the position of women suffered accordingly (Prenzler and Wimshurst 1997).

- The Second World War saw women police once again being charged with the guardianship of the nation's morals where they were expected to exert a restraining influence on women's sexual behaviour. They themselves also became the object of policemen's (legitimate) affections with a view to marriage. However, by the 1960s they were also portrayed as being the subject of policemen's illegitimate sexual fantasies. Women were represented as sexually attractive and available as women but ineffectual as police officers. Women who might be conceived as handling the rough and tough tasks of policing are represented as emasculating and unattractive.
- There was also a loss of innocence in the sense that during the early period, women were simply thought to be ignorant of, or untouched by the taint of association with, criminals and sexual crime. Yet this very fact, emphasizing the unlikely prospect of a policewoman, was the *raison d'être* used by the police to deploy women in potentially dangerous undercover work. Women presented themselves as action orientated, riding motor cycles, flying aeroplanes, whereas male writers' and cartoonists' portrayal of policewomen before the Second World War presented them as ineffectual and side-tracked by emotional entanglements. After the War, representations become more explicit, with sex being used knowingly by policewomen, directed at both male police officers and offenders.

Integration

A further significant catalyst for the advancement of women in policing has been equal opportunities legislation. Again, dates and details vary but the principle of integrated policing being established by law is common. In the United States, the 1963 Equal Pay Act and the 1972 Title VII Amendment to the Civil Rights Act of 1964 prohibited discrimination on grounds of race, colour, religion, sex or national origin. Implementation involved the setting of hiring quotas and affirmative action programmes, although Schulz (1995a, p. 134) suggests it was as much fiscal as political pressures resulting from the Revenue Sharing Act that prompted jurisdictions to comply with equality employment requirements. Prenzler (1992) reports that in Australia, rapid expansion in numbers of women police followed the introduction of anti-discrimination legislation, although in the immediate aftermath, only some Australian states have introduced part-time working, and grievance procedures to handle sexual harassment. Little was initially done by way of affirmative action programmes. It was not until the introduction of such programmes, certainly in New South Wales police, that women police roles expanded (Sutton 1992).

In Britain, the Metropolitan Police anticipated the equality legislation of 1975 (Sex Discrimination Act). Change was driven very much from the top by Commissioner Sir Robert Mark and Commander Shirley Becke (Weinberger 1995). But integration was at a price. Becke (1973) writes: 'Like anyone else women police cannot have their cake and eat it. Equality must be paid for by the giving up of privilege...They had their own department dealing with personnel matters and a good deal of time and effort went into dealing with these things. Equality means this must go'. Police unions had 'unstable' relationships with women officers. In Poland (Trzcinska 1997, personal communication) and in Australia (Prenzler 1998) police unions took an early proactive stance but later became negative and even obstructive. Attitude change was not immediately forthcoming from Britain's Police Federation whose response to equality legislation was to make a case for the exemption of the police. The Federation confidently pronounced that the very nature of the duties of a police constable is contrary to all that is finest and best in women (Whitaker 1979, p. 120). Letters to *Police Review* and *Police* (Police Federation of England and Wales' official magazine) and reports of Federation Conferences reflect a paternalistic concern but also a new sense of combative, if not aggressive patriarchal opposition:

> I can foresee the time when a young female colleague is going to be raped. If you can live with that on your conscience I cannot (Ian Westwood, Greater Manchester, *Police*, June 1978).

> Let us keep the ladies in their proper place. Pay them the same and give them the same conditions, but let them do the woman's work and relieve us of it (Mr Fairfield, Warwickshire, *Police*, June 1976).

Men feared women would gain a short cut to promotion and 'having obtained this short cut to inspector there is then nothing to stop them getting on the equality bandwagon and ending up as senior officers in charge of men.' (Letter, *Police Review*, 22 August 1975). This had been the fear of the anonymous writer to Police

Review in 1933 if 'Eve' was to be permitted to work within the Criminal Investigation Department. The commentaries become more offensive, with a return to lesbian conspiracies of the 1920s as the eponymous MC Pigg writing in the Police Federation Magazine *Police* (7 September 1974, p. 24) illustrates: 'Of course we have the odd out and out suffragette. Harmless, that's what we thought they were. Cheerfully abandoning any claims to femininity and the making the best of nature's injustices – my name's really Jennifer but Jeff will do – all string vests and Old Spice.'

And cartoons become even more sexually explicit. *Police* 1974 publishes a drawing of a policeman on top of a policewoman in the back seat of a police car with the caption 'Are you committed zero-three? Over'. Whilst the representation of policemen's opposition is increasing in hostility, women officers defend the specialist skills of the policewomen's department but on grounds reminiscent of old logic. The 'good' policewoman is there not so much to protect women but rather to preserve the reputation of her male colleague:

> Are you saying to me that the experience we have built up should be wasted...I am talking about specialisation that has been thrown out of the window... [People] want us to see their daughters. We should be there so that you men are not getting allegations made against you...Nothing upsets me more than some little trollop that we deal with turning round and saying that a PC did this, that and the other, simply because there was't a policewoman there (Miss Henderson, Durham Police, *Police*, 8 June 1976).

Moral worth of policewomen was still to be a significant characteristic in their recruitment to the service (Walklate 1992). Walklate reports the results of a study looking at the references provided for applicants to the police and discovered 'intelligence and sense of humour were qualities only attributed to male applicants and that good moral values dedicated and reliable were qualities only attributed to female applicants' (p. 228). These findings are taken as supportive evidence that the police service still reflects a patriarchal concern to control women by controlling their sexuality 'a process which is as effectively sustained by women...as it is by men' (Walklate 1992, p. 231).

There was now an interesting divergence in the official rhetoric as illustrated by the views of HMIC in Scotland and England and Wales a year after the passing of SDA: 'Achievements of women in the past year have done much to dispel the earlier misgivings about their deployment in every type of duty' (HMIC,

England and Wales 1976, p. 4). 'The failure to achieve complete success [in the integration of women officers] is not for want of trying on the part of the management but is due solely to the physical unsuitability of women to cope with the drunken violent hooligan particularly in rough areas on night duty' (HMIC, Scotland 1976, p. 16).

Women's physical attractiveness was still an issue. During the 1950s and 60s, recruitment of women officers to the police in Glasgow required candidates to be of good physique such that the recruiting inspector writes of the 'splendid' appearance of some of the candidates (Strathclyde Police Archive Mitchell Library). In March 1979, *Police Review* was running a competition to find the prettiest policewoman in the land. In Holland in 1981, women officers were acting as majorettes during official occasions. The *Australian Federal Police Journal* was carrying cartoons of attractive policewomen clearly distracting male officers. One appearing in December 1984 has a police vehicle crashed into a tree with the woman officer saying to the male driver 'At least your different, all

Source: Australian, Federal Police Journal, December 1984, p. 159.

the others run out of petrol.' In 1995, the Hungary Police organized a Ms Hungarian Policewoman competition (Brown 1997). In the 1990s, Belgian policewomen were acting as hostesses for official functions (Rinsema 1996, p. 9). Newspaper reports of women officers in post communist Russia draw attention to women's attractiveness. 'Alla...the 28 year old member of the St Petersburg SWAT team is beautiful and strongly built, intelligent and thoughtful. Through her helmet you catch a glimpse of green eyes with rare orange sparkles' (*St Petersburg Times*, March, 21–27 1995).

What is of interest is the apparent time lag in the emergence of devices emphasizing women's visual appearance (display value) that diminishes their value as professional police officers at different points in time. Not only this, but demeaning cartoons of policewomen were not confined to police magazines. *The Police Surgeon* of 15 April 1979 carried the following cartoon, incidentally printed next to an article about the sensitive handling of examination of rape victims. The male doctor is clearly waiting to examine a patient. To one side is a disreputable looking hippy whilst on the other side is a naked woman. A smirking police sergeant, indicating the hippy, is saying 'This one's for the examination Sir. That one's WPC 1212.'

By the 1980s some changes in presentation were discernible. In 1987, *Police Review* was carrying articles and front cover pictures of serving women officers with their children (*Police Review*, 30 January 1987, 31 August 1990) and there even appeared a photograph of a pregnant woman officer in a maternity uniform (13 August 1993). Yet unofficially, attitudes were less progressive. Suzanne Box won a sex discrimination claim against the Metropolitan Police concerning blocked promotion. She was pregnant when applying for the rank of sergeant and was discounted on the grounds of a part-time mentality because of her pregnancy (*Daily Mail*, 7 Febuary 1995). In 1997, there was an outcry as officers from one UK force had invited a stripper dressed as a policewoman to a party at police headquarters in which behaviour of officers invited several formal complaints (*News of the World*, 16 February).

Gregory (1987) considers that appeals to European law have not been successful in improving women's position in the workforce in the various countries of the European Union. That may be so in the early years: for example, the Minister of Defence in Belgium used European law to exclude women from the Gendarmerie (Rijkswacht) because it was believed that the work was 'too physically and morally risky' (Hazenberg and Ormiston 1995). However, the Garda Siochana was obliged to lift its exemption from the Employment Equality Act in 1985 because of European Directive SI331.

In Eastern Europe under communism, state socialism effected equality for all citizens so there was no specific equality legislation. Subhan (1996, p. 15) argues that under communism, women encountered much the same impediments within the labour market as women in the non-communist world. Moreover, since the collapse of the Eastern bloc much pre-communist gender stereotyping has resurfaced. In a developmental exchange visit to Slovakia, Leonard *et al.* (1991, p. 146) quotes a local police commander's response to the idea of operationally active policewomen: 'policemen would simply gaze at them all the time and not do their work'.

In trying to explain the communist notion of equality Trzcinska (1997, personal communication) explained that this was based on a concept of 'equal stomachs'. This means that both men and women have to eat and should have equal access to resources (salaries) in order to buy food. Trzcinska also explains there was a kind of 'false modesty' in which people, particularly women, did not openly show their ambition for promotion. There were very few women in the Eastern European police forces.

In Australia, Prenzler (1994) argues that whilst legislation did accelerate the recruitment of women into the police, litigation acted as a fillip to recalcitrant States. In 1980, a rejected woman applicant took the New South Wales Police to the Anti-discrimination Board on the grounds that an illegal quota system was in place. The quota system was subsequently removed, as was the marriage bar in 1981 after a woman applicant successfully challenged her rejection on the grounds that she was married.

Recourse to litigation in Britain is rare but perhaps because of this, when cases occur they attract considerable attention. Wendy de Launay brought an early successful case when a supervisor returned her to foot patrol duties believing that her being partnered with a male colleague in a patrol car adversely affected morale. Assistant Chief Constable Alison Halford brought a sex discrimination claim in 1990 that she had been passed over for promotion on the grounds of her sex. Her motivation was that she realised her own career would go no further but she wished to make a point for the benefit of other women: 'I accepted that it was the end of my career. I didn't want to muck it up for other women' (reported by James David Smith 1993).

The issue of Miss Halford's sexuality was brought up in an effort to discredit her. Smith reports how the chairman of the Police Authority, George Bundred, claimed that she was a lesbian and that this was bad for discipline in the force (p. 33). Not only this but that other members of the Authority were disturbed by her resorting to litigation and that 'a humbler approach might have been more appropriate' (p. 34). These discrediting devices look remarkably like the ones deployed in the 1920s referred to earlier by Macready and Dunning when undermining the efforts of the WPV. When later, two women did reach the rank of chief constable, they tended to play down the gender card and emphasized their promotion on the grounds of merit. (*Police Review*, 7 July 1995, 13 December 1996). Susan Davies, when head of higher training for the police in England and Wales, somewhat ruefully declared there to be too few role models to support women officers (Davies 1994, p. 26).

The history of women's entry into policing in the United States was marked by open and widespread sexual harassment and discrimination. Prenzler (1992) notes that women were often denied back-up, were the subject of jokes, pranks, sexual innuendo and propositions, were denied locker facilities and subject to capricious application of rules. A series of studies were commissioned to examine the suitability and efficacy of women officers in a range of policing functions (see Lunneborg 1989). Women became defensive in the light of the questions being asked about them: 'Are policewomen doing a good job? How well are policewomen doing a man's job?' (Van Wormer 1980, p. 41) On the one hand, women were being asked to resocialize themselves in order to behave aggressively as police officers, on the other, women were seen as an antidote to 'muscularity', a source of citizen complaint and corrupt practice (Sherman 1975). Lanier (1996) described these officers as the pioneers who faced conflicts of role and expectations. They responded by flight or fight. This was manifest in either acceptance of a subordinated role or, if unable to face the difficulties, resignation from the police. A few of the women in the immediate post-integration period chose to challenge the traditional male dominance. As a result, they had to put up with minor irritations and serious indignities as they sought to play an equal role with their male officer colleagues. In coping with their newly integrated roles, Grennan (1987) suggested that women officers developed an aggressiveness in an effort to match their 'macho' male peers. Within this category is 'the dyke' (Hunt 1990) who is perceived as overtly man-like who walks, talks and acts in an aggressive and tough manner. The second response was to retreat to a passive femininity. Martin (1980) describes police*woman* as unassertive, holding few career expectation, acknowleding the physical limitations of women officers and struggling to maintain her female gender role. Martin (1990) reports a diminution of overt hostility with the passage of equal opportunities legislation and procedures for handling harassment.

Despite some advances, as women encroached into more operational spheres, there has been evidence of a resurgence of rhetoric to counter the application of equal opportunities within the police that look depressingly familiar. In 1996, *Police Review* (20 September) illustrated an article entitled 'equality trap' with a drawing of the grim reaper holding an equal opportunities policy in its hands, signifying the death of the traditional police service. The introduction of the long or side handled baton to both men and women officers in the early 1990s replaced the tradition truncheon of the 'British Bobby'. A *Police Review* cartoon of May 1994 sees a large policewoman wearing a protective breast plate with exaggerated

'If she wants to call it a baton, who are we to argue?'

Source: *Police Review*, 6 May 1994, p. 8.

spikes as nipples carrying a pair of pinchers advancing on some hapless male constable (intent on castration) being greeted with 'if she wants to call it a baton, who are we to argue'.

The finding that women officers in the UK outachieve their male counterparts in promotion examinations, Objective Structured Performance Related Examination (OSPRE), prompted a cartoon in *Police Review* (July 1997) in which two officers faced with the question 'which is the best washing powder to remove blood stains from the store detective's pink cotton blouse' sees the woman writing her answer and the man staring at the questions surrounded by crumbled sheets of paper. The ambivalence of the police organization towards equal opportunities is evident in the ambiguity of the cartoon. On the one hand, such a domestic question as relevant to assess the competency of senior officers for the modern police force might indicate the emasculating consequences of equality policies. On the other hand, the obvious relish with which the woman officer is writing her answer locates her firmly within the domestic sphere where she is obviously more comfortable.

Thus in bringing our analysis up to date we conclude:

- The integration of women in policing has largely been achieved through the force of law in the form of equality legislation rather than desire for reform or social justice from within police organizations. Progress tends to have been made through the courageous efforts of individual litigants. The personal cost of undertaking litigation is high, with litigants reporting symptoms of stress associated with the legal process in addition to the experience they complain of (*Guardian*, 9 October 1996).
- Models of equality were based on liberal rather than radical philosophies. In other words, equality was to open up areas previously restricted to women but on the basis that women *should do the job like the men*. This spawned a spate of comparative studies to determine how well women undertook patrol work. The assessment was based on a male model. There was little reflective analysis concerning the nature of policing and an optimization of qualities of men and women within a philosophy of equal but different equality policies.
- Women have attempted to come to terms with the male-dominated police culture in a number of ways. Research studies suggest that they seek approval, adapt or accommodate by adopting an aggressive style thereby 'becoming one of the boys'

(Bryant, Dunkerley and Kelland 1985). Alternatively 'they resist the adoption and performance of occupational traits that are masculine' (Brewer 1991b, p. 241) preferring to retain as much femininity as the occupational culture will allow. Both strategies are costly. The latter often attracts sexual harassment which the officer is trying to avoid and such officers are perceived as loners and ineffectual. The overly masculinized women officers also face denigration for their loss of femininity and/or are perceived as man hating. These judgments map directly onto the representations of women officers alluded to at the beginning of this chapter from the *Punch* and *Illustrated London News* cartoons.

- The denigration of policewomen continues to be made through a discourse of sexuality drawn from the official and unofficial sources. The originating rhetoric of humour was employed to demonstrate the ludicrous notion of women as police officers based on their physical frailty and sexual dangerousness. Representations of the unlikely proposition of a woman police officer presented her as 'unnatural' and mannish. Thus the historical discourse was deployed to both deprofessionalize and defeminize women police. The rationale adopted for legitimizing women's entry into the police was on the grounds of women being better able to control the sexuality of other women. Thus women were demarcated into specific forms of policing and expected to adopt an acquiescence that mirrored broader societal gender roles and expectations. This harnessed 'natural' caring and nurturing roles of women. It was likely then that such women would be represented as potential marriage partners for policemen. Challenges to these presumptions were represented as 'unnatural' implying the unavailability or undesirability of women officers; that is the women must either be gay or ugly (or both). The devices used to preserve these representations included the explicit eroticization of policewomen through cartoons, comments, letters, debates. Over time, the manifest character of the imagery has changed but the underlying purpose to deprofessionalize or defeminize women remains the same.
- Examples of emphasis on women's visual attractiveness can be found from different police jurisdictions, at different times. As earlier attempts to use policewomen to control other women's (sexual) conduct undermined their own claims to femininity, policewomen find that being used as display objects serve to undermine their claims to professionalism.

4

The Contemporary Picture: Constants and Contrasts

Introduction

The previous chapter engaged an historical frame through which to pursue and unravel the discourses used to represent policewomen. We revealed the origins, sedimentation and reactivation of rhetorical devices, such as scurrilous humour, satire and appeals to 'nature', used to maintain the proposition that policing is an unsuitable job for a woman and which results in deprofessionalization and/or defeminization of women officers. Rhetorical devices also include praise supporting women engaged in segregated duties, to do with women and children and controlling sexual behaviour of other women, acting as a justification for the entry of women into the police and legitimation of restricting their roles to an extended domestic sphere. Informal comment, cartoons and official discourses serve to keep women in their place by sexualizing them. This is akin to a sexuality paradigm, discussed by Halford, Savage and Witz (1997, p. 228), which articulates the notion that certain organizational discourses control women through denigrating or praising social constructions. We located examples of these processes in the Anglo-American and European traditions of police organizations.

Commentators of post equality-legislation policing vary in their interpretation of the present position of women police officers. Wimshurst (1995, p. 6) suggests that some analysts find support for the continuation of male antagonism towards women officers whilst others note changes in and improvement of attitudes, especially in younger policemen, partly as a consequence of equality policies (Martin 1997). This chapter provides a cross-sectional examination of women's current position in the police.

Here we draw upon what has been termed the 'gender paradigm' (Halford, Savage and Witz 1997, p. 228) which relates to the notion that corporate patriarchy and systemic relations sustain male dominance and female subordination and the contingent approach (Halford, Savage and Witz 1997, pp. 6–10) as exemplified by the work of Rosabeth Kanter. Specifically, we examine the structural properties and mechanisms that sustain the distributions of men and women hierarchically and laterally within the organization and the impact of this on policing and women in policing.

Organizational structures

Surveys conducted by the European Network of Police Women (Hazenberg and Ormiston 1995) show that average percentages of women police range from 4 per cent (Portugal, Belgium) 6 per cent (Denmark) 8 per cent (Germany, Hungary) 12 per cent (Netherlands) to 13 per cent (Sweden). Australia and the United States have approximately the same percentage (about 15 per cent) of women officers as the UK (Brown 1998). Marshall (1998, p. 77) in a study of 32 countries found 13 per cent to be the average of women's share of policing personnel. These percentages reflect the the token presence of women within most police organizations, especially at very senior rank. There are no women officers in the three highest police grades in Denmark, Ireland or Portugal. Relatively few countries (Sweden, UK, United States) have women at chief officer rank. Unusually, in France the percentage share of women increases as the rank of officer rises (Maniloff 1998). In May 1997, French policewomen represented 7.7 per cent of constables, 9.2 per cent of inspectors and 10.1 per cent of superintendents.

Martin (1989b p. 324) reviews research studies from other organizational settings to show contradictory findings resulting from predictions from the Kanter thesis that as numbers rise, discriminatory treatment should decline. Martin cites the work of South who concluded that increases in numbers, without alterations in the relations between dominants and tokens, is not likely to improve the position for minorities: rather, it is likely to make matters worse. Ott (1989, p. 42) deploys the critical-mass argument to explain this finding. This idea suggests that a majority will resist a minority as the minority grows in numbers towards parity. This is because the majority will lose their superior status and privileged access to power and other organizational rewards. Several research studies can help us determine the outcome for policewomen of the predictions that increasing numbers will have a beneficial transformative effect, make no difference, or increase discriminatory behaviour.

Wertsch (1998) undertook a small-scale qualitative study of US police officers to examine the impact of tokenism. She found that the policewomen in her study who conformed to definition as tokens did indeed suffer from exclusion in terms of mentoring, after-work socializing and were the subject of gossip and rumour. Moreover, the operating of stereotyping created pressures of 'role entrapment'. This is where women found themselves pushed into what were considered gender-appropriate deployments such as sexual assaults, community programmes and drug-awareness projects and excluded from non-sexual-violence calls. These were justified on grounds of service delivery and protection. Wertsch (1998, p. 53) concludes from her study that in the researched police department, the strength of the dynamics of tokenism overcame the organization's equality policies and did result in inhibiting women from applying for promotion. Moreover women were found to retreat to 'token sanctuaries' where they felt reasonably comfortable but out of which they did not wish to venture. Wertsch argues that this represents strategic self-positioning and should be distinguished from the women's ghettos identified by Martin (1989a) which are support positions or operation task compatible with stereotyped female roles.

A study of Dutch police officers conducted by Ott (1989) not only finds support for the discriminatory treatment of token policewomen but also the diminution of discrimination when women were present in larger numbers (over the 15 per cent threshold in specific teams). Token policewomen were more likely to perceive themselves as vulnerably visible, experience stronger stereotypic work deployments, were more often absent from work because of the stress engendered by male colleagues' behaviour and endured more sexual harassment than women working in groups that had more women. Women in these teams are less likely to feel isolated, experience harassment and are more likely to be accepted by policemen.

Wimshurst's (1995) study of recruits to Australian police forces indicated that despite greater employment of women officers, there was no evidence of major changes. There was little apparent difference between men and women recruits in terms of how they viewed their roles as police officers. Felkenes and Lasley (1992) examined the impact of an affirmative action programme in the Los Angeles Police Department (LAPD). This had come about as the consequence of the Blake consent decree in 1979 whereby the LAPD was required to increase the proportion of women officers to 20 per cent and black and Hispanic officers to a representative percentage as reflected in the LA standard Metropolitan Statistical Area projections. Findings indicated no differences in job satisfaction of officers or levels of organizational commitment or motivations in seeking police careers. Nor was there any evidence of changes in levels of intercolleague hostility. Worden (1993) undertook a secondary data analysis of men and women in US police departments and found relatively few differences between men and women officers, although she concedes that the original data on which the study was based were somewhat dated (1977). Steel and Lovrich (1987) evaluated the impact of having more or fewer women in policing on crime rates, clear-up rates and costs of police operations in several American cities. They found no differences on any of the evaluative dimensions between cities that hired the most or least policewomen.

In a study of British women police officers, Brown (1998) attempted a direct test of the proposition that as numbers of women increase then harassment should decrease. In this study, the percentage of women working in specific areas of police specialism were calculated.

A sample of policewomen working in these areas were surveyed and asked about the levels of sexual harassment they experienced. A mean score of the total amount of harassment from different sources was calculated. By and large, the percentage of women compared to men appeared to have a negligible effect on the rates of harassment reported. Brown (1998) suggests that the dynamics at work here are more complicated than simply numbers and have to do with the status of the specialist area, numbers of senior staff within the area of policing (as opposed to largely unsupervised patrol) and recognition of specialist expertize overriding gender differentials.

Figure 4   Percentage of women officers and levels of harassment
experienced

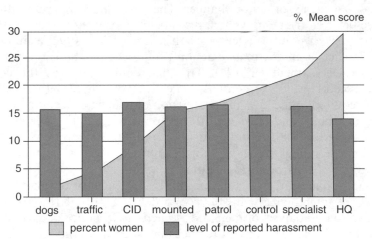

Source: Adapted from Brown (1998, p. 273).

Impact on police women of informal occupational culture

Acceptance

Despite their having been involved in law enforcement since before
World War I, American policewomen still find being fully accepted
by male colleagues problematic. Janus, Janus, Lord and Power
(1988) reported that only 8 per cent of policewomen felt fully
accepted by their male colleagues whilst 62 per cent thought they
were mostly accepted. In a survey of Ohio policewomen, Youngblood (1993) found that only 1 per cent of policewomen felt they
were fully accepted by male colleagues with 20 per cent indicating
they were mostly accepted, 53 per cent somewhat accepted and 31
per cent that they were accepted with difficulty. Daum (1994)
reported that 42 per cent of policewomen from a municipal department did not feel accepted by male officers and 55 per cent reported
that they were not accepted by male supervisors. Lunneborg (1989)
reviews the reasons for this continued lack of acceptance which is
related to performance capabilities: women were still perceived by
men to be better at handling matters dealing with women and

children and sexual offences and were less likely to be thought able to manage violent situations or back up male officers when confronting violence. Women are also still perceived to be physically in capable of handling all police tasks (Daum 1994). Similar attitudes are reported in surveys of police forces in Scotland (Wilkie and Currie 1989), England (Coffey, Brown and Savage 1992), New Zealand (Waugh 1994), Australia (French and Waugh 1998) and Canada (Walker 1993).

However there are some indications of change. Gossett and Williams (1998, p. 68), in a qualitative study of a South West American Metropolitan police department, noted:

> there was a consensus among the women interviewed that law enforcement has changed with the times, that discrimination of the past is not present in the same form today. Discrimination as perceived today is subtle and less overt than in the past. [However] even while acknowledging progress, the majority of female officers, almost two thirds, perceived discrimination against women in law enforcement today.

Trzcinska (1996) indicates that Polish women officers are scarcely tolerated by their male colleagues. She writes 'even when uniform was assigned, women were treated as decorative and office material. In a skirt and on high heels it is difficult to catch the bus, so pursuing a criminal is certainly out of the question'. The prejudices of Polish policemen look remarkably like those of their Western European counterparts. Trzcinska (1998, personal communication) suggests, however, there to be not only a decline in women recruits into police training but also return of the mentality that women are better at home having babies and looking after the family.

Gütges (1998) paints a not dissimilar picture of the experience for women officers in former DDR German States (Brandenburg, Mecklenberg-Vorpommern, Sachsen, Sachsen-Anhalt and Thüringen). From interviews with women officers who worked in these States before and after Unification, she reports an improvement in recruitment practices although provision of child care has declined. Women, however, saw no differences in their occupance of management positions in the DDR and New States:

> management positions are rarely given to women and there is very little change today. The women see the reason for that in the dual role they are expected to fulfil, that of working wife and mother. Women who have a family are worn out doing two jobs. Men with a family tend to rely on their wives to take care of

children. The results of this traditional approach is that men are able to spend
more time and effort developing their careers, whereas the women are morally
expected to remain at home at the expense of their own careers

Policewomen also report that men persist in their prejudices about
their potential as managers and that there is an absence of role
models in the workplace. In terms of their experience of sexual
harassment, many indicated that they did not consider sexual jokes
or obscene comments as harassment: rather, that women employed
in a culture dominated by men should accept such remarks.

Sexual harassment

In the early 1990s, several studies had revealed high levels of sexual
harassment occurring within forces in England and Wales (Young
1991; Anderson, Brown and Campbell 1993; HMIC 1992). These
suggested an endemic sexism in which 'nine out of ten police women
sometimes or often hear sexually explicit comments or suggestive
jokes about women' (Anderson, Brown and Campbell 1993, p. 81)
with policemen being 'overtly and consistently hostile towards
women in "the job"' (Young 1991, p. 193). In an unpublished
paper, Young (1996) itemizes some of the epithets used to describe
women officers: split arse, treacle (tart), slapper, bitch, turtle, P.I.K.
(Pig in knickers). HMIC for England and Wales recognized the
'serious problem of sexual harassment' (HMIC 1992, p. 16) within
the service. In 1998, a former Thames Valley detective, Dee Mazur-
kiewicz successfully pursued a sexual harassment claim. She
described, amongst her experiences, being nicknamed 'massive
cleavage' – a pun on her surname (*Police Review*, 22 May 1998).
In addition, she described in a radio interview (23 November 1998)
how her sergeant claimed that she obtained successful confessions
from suspects because 'you get your boobs out'. Fellow officers
gossiped about how she had sex with the criminal fraternity in
order to achieve her impressive clear-up rate. Her descriptions of
the attitudes and behaviour of her male superior officers and colleagues hark back to the claims made in the 1940s and 1950s
discussed in the previous chapter.

Not all surveys report finding examples of sexual harassment. In
a thematic inspection on equal opportunities within Scottish Police
Forces, Her Majesty's Inspectorate of Constabulary reported that

'female officers commented during pre inspection on having seen reports of the findings in England and Wales did not recognise the culture said to be prevalent there' (p.17). The Inspection concluded that if acceptable banter overstepped the mark, 'where female officers did not intervene other male officers would be quick to do so on her behalf' (HMIC 1993, p. 17). Moreover, the low incidence of unacceptable behaviours was accounted for by 'the strong influence of Scottish religious tradition.' and teamwork, bringing about 'a healthy atmosphere between colleagues of the opposites sex' (p. 18).

Other jurisdictions within the British Isles do report high levels of sexual harassment. A survey conducted within the RUC reported that 'a high proportion of female officers had suffered some form of harassment' (HMIC 1997, p. 28). Stalker (1988, p. 68) had described language used by RUC policemen when referring to HQ-based policewomen reminiscent of that reported by Young (1991): 'bitch squad, the hen house or cow shed'. A more recent study by Brewer (1991b, p. 237) concluded that RUC policewomen felt they were 'fair game as sex objects', and that policewomen 'have jokes made about their bodies, have to listen to dirty jokes, have passes made at them, and are the subject to some sexual harassment from low-level officers (having their waists pinched, arms put round them, comments made as to their appearance)'. Burman and Lloyd (1993, p. 38) reported that Scottish women officers engaged in child protection work were referred to as 'the fanny squad, the nappy squad, and the women's and weans group'.

There is little evidence available on the existence of a macho police culture in the Garda Siochana. McCullagh (1996, p. 151) concludes that 'in the absence of the relevant research we do not know the extent to which such a sub culture can be found among gardai.' However, O'Mahony (1996, p. 131) demonstrates that since the late-1980s, there has been a severe crises of moral, mission and identity and concludes. 'Relations between Garda and its community have been seriously damaged – perhaps permanently – by the headlong rush into a macho attitude to crime fighting, by the infatuation with machinery and technology and by the abandonment of, or at least the devaluation of, the old priorities of community service.'

There is evidence for the presence of sexual harassment in Belgium (Corryn 1994), Denmark (Ibsen Froslee, cited in Hazenberg and Ormiston 1995) and Holland (Eikenaar 1993). In the United States, the occurrence of sexual harassment is reported by Daum

(1994), Jacobs (1988), Pendergrass and Ostrove (1984), Wexler and Logan (1983).

Kersten (1996) suggests a link between reported rates of sexual assault and the rise in sexual assault victimization. Kersten proposes that the particularly virulent form of 'aggressive masculinity' in Australia means that violence as the way to resolve disputes is condoned. Kersten concludes (1996, p. 391):

> the extreme visibility of Australia's 'uncontrollable and dangerous' men has to be deciphered against a background of a deep social, cultural, and economic crisis on the fifth continent which has repercussions for gender relations. The seemingly self evident construct of an Australian 'national masculinity' with an emphasis on physical prowess and independence is crumbling.

As a result, Kersten, argues Australian men compensate by using practices reliant on physical strength where the weaker and despised object, women, children and homosexuals, are dehumanized and victimized. In other words, physical and sexual assault become facts of daily life acting to compensate for losses in hegemonic masculinity. Since the police represents 'an almost pure form of hegemonic masculinity' (Fielding 1994, p. 47) there is no reason to suppose that Australian women police officers are not subjected to sexual harassment. This was indeed found to be the case by Sutton (1996) who reports levels higher to that found in the UK and Holland.

Women's career aspirations

Meagher and Yentes (1986) reported few differences in what motivated men or women in becoming police officers. Weishart (1987) found US men were more likely to indicate job security and women to providing a needed service as their primary motives for joining the police. Poole and Pogrebin (1988) found with length of service, women were less likely to indicate career advancement as their motive for remaining in the police service.

Whilst there appears to be little difference between what motivates men and women managers to become managers (Alimo-Metcalfe 1993), there is a suggestion of gender difference between management styles in general (Jago and Vroom 1982) and in the police in particular (Price 1974). The former observation suggest, that women are more participative and make more use of group

discussions than men; the latter found that women police exe
exhibited higher scores than male executives on emot
independence, verbal aggression, conservatism, concern w
appearance and social roles. Women have been found to operate
with different communicative styles. Stuart (1994) suggests when a
woman communicates a problem to a man, he is likely to try and
solve it. She may simply wish to explore alternatives. The man may
then be frustrated by this apparent irrelevant diversion into, say,
issues about how people may respond to the various available
options, instead of dealing purely with facts. Stuart goes further
and demonstrates how research finds that men focus on external
issues and prefer to exchange hard information. Women talk to
establish or reinforce a personal connection, or exchange experience. In the workplace, this means that women are more prepared to
share power and information For men, information represents
power and status.

A number of studies conducted within the United Kingdom
provides some evidence of movement in terms of women's career
aspirations. In 1987, Morris (1987, p. 143) showed that fewer
women compared with men expressed promotion aspirations (50
compared to 80 per cent). Morcover, a third of women felt that the
1975 Sex Discrimination Act had worsened their promotion
chances. This is actually so in percentage terms. Examination of
police establishment figures from Her Majesty's Inspectorate of
Constabulary annual reports show that in 1970, about 16 per cent
of women held supervisory rank as a function of all policewomen.
This was five years before equality legislation when women served in
separate departments. The equivalent percentage for men was 25
per cent. By 1980, five years after the SDA, women's proportionate
share of supervisory rank had dropped to about 7 per cent, a
proportion that has remained stable since. The proportionate
share of men holding supervisory rank has not changed. Brown
(1998) reports data that actually showed a drop in the proportionate
share that women held of supervisory rank in London's Metropolitan Police. However, other data, taking into account the loss
of supervisory rank due to organizational changes and managerial
reforms in the British police, showed that the percentage share of
senior rank for men had declined whilst that for women remained
stable (Brown and Gillick 1998). The proportionate share for
women was still less than half of that for men and had not returned
to pre-equal-opportunity legislation levels.

Allen (1997) provided some results from one British police force, Bedfordshire, showing about the same percentage of men and women officers considering promotion unimportant (58 per cent of women and 54 per cent of men respectively) whilst about a third of both men and women thought promotion important. Holdaway and Parker (1998) report results from another British police force and show that 44 per cent of men and 61 per cent of women thought promotion important (although differences were not statistically different when controlling for age of officers). Of interest were differences in reasons given for being promoted. Men were more likely to indicate job security and higher pay (instrumental motives) while women mentioned opportunities for advancement and challenging work (intrinsic motives). Thus, the aspirational gap between men and women appears to be closing with movement in both directions, that is, more women and fewer men indicating a desire to achieve higher rank. However, there is still a gap between men and women in actually activating promotion campaigns. Results from Allen's (1997) survey reported that only 34 per cent of women had taken promotional examinations compared to 47 per cent of men. There appeared to be little difference between the men and women in terms of their analysis of inhibitions in wishing for or achieving promotion: cliques operating in traffic and CID such that 'if your face does not fit' you will not succeed; restricted opportunities in a new climate of delayering ranks and restructuring. However, women were marginally more likely to cite lack of motivation or experience as stopping them from applying and were more responsive to help in studying compared with men.

In her comparative analysis of British and American police officers, Heidensohn (1992, p. 63) concluded, with the passing of anti-discriminatory laws in both the US and UK, theoretically at least, women should have been able to apply for promotion on equal terms with male officers. The situation was rather better in the United States than in Britain. In particular, Heidensohn observed a greater degree of confidence and sense of achievement to characterize senior women officers in America than in Britain (p. 64). Nonetheless, for women in both jurisdictions, Heidensohn felt there to be 'a huge, if shadowy presence which hangs like a miasma over this whole matter. Since the 1970s, all manner of indicators have suggested fine weather and fair passage for women in policing. In practice, the ship is still in troubled waters' (p. 65). She remarks on the repetitive cycle of harassment and abuse that beset the career progression of women in policing. Is there scope for a more optimistic reading in the light of new research findings?

In a national study of sex discrimination within police forces in England and Wales conducted in 1992, Brown, Campbell and Fife Schaw (1995) found no differences between men and women in terms of dissatisfaction with their rank although now, it was marginally more men (43 per cent) that felt they were not competing for promotion on equal terms compared with women. Scott (1997), reporting the results of another national sample of serving British police officers, also found no gender differences in satisfaction with current rank. Rank aspirations at the beginning of police careers were the same for men and women; although, more men aspired to higher rank compared to women when asked about their current promotion target (18 per cent of women set this at superintendent, compared to 27 per cent of men). Scott's results showed that men on average make twice as many applications as women for higher rank. Scott found that women were more likely than men to cite lack of organizational or supervisor support and insufficient time to study. Women were also more responsive than men to taking advantage of schemes to help their promotion chances: networking; practice boards; secondments; regular career-developing interviews; career planning; and confidence-building courses. Following equality legislation, it appears that women have raised their aspirations for higher rank, but that a gap remains between men and women in terms of their activating their promotion trajectories. Coffey, Brown and Savage (1992) suggest that a possible reason for this is a reluctance to either become the pioneer that breaks into a level not previously enjoyed by a woman, or being a solo woman in a supervisory rank. This may activate the token dynamics alluded to earlier. Lunneborg (1989, p. 153) notes the experiences of Penny Harrington as chief of police in Portland, Oregon. Lunneborg writes:

> In spite of the fact that she tried to implement a value-based participatory style of management and for the first time in over ten years had weekly staff meetings with the deputy chiefs and captains, she was charged with failing to consult with top commanders. In spite of sending new narcotics officers away to school for special training and creating a new drugs unit, she was charged with damaging the department's drug enforcement capability...Harrington instituted a number of policies to open up channels of communication, but she was said to display an unyielding management style.

Similar criticizms have been levelled at Pauline Clare, Britain's first woman chief constable. The formal inspection of the force noted that there had been rapid change such that 'members of the support staff have only a vague idea of where they fit into the new structures, or what the future will hold'; reservations were expressed about reorganization in respect of detective, traffic and criminal justice departments (HMIC 1998, p. 7) The Inspectorate especially noted 'not all those who criticize strands of the change programme should be viewed as having closed minds, people past their sell by date who are reluctanct to face change... there has been a management failure to implement change without the most careful assessment of how this will impact at street level'.

Another problem for women senior officers can be inferred from Watson's (1992, p. 198) critique of femocratic leadership: that the femocrat sells out in response to perks of their position; conformist pressures not to tell it as it is; being maligned or misunderstood. Not only are there too few role models, but senior women may not want to become a symbolic class action whereby their individual success is a signal for the success of women operating at senior level. Although Silvestri (personal communication), in some preliminary analysis of an incomplete study of senior women police officers, suggests there to be little evidence of femocratic advocacy as a leadership style among policewomen in Britain, Holdaway and Parker (1998) found, from a study of one British force, that officers having the most liberal views about women and their careers were higher-ranked women officers.

One of the few published studies of women supervisory officers discusses the difficulties facing US women sergeants (Wexler and Quinn 1985). Whilst men and women did not differ in terms of the identification of their training needs, men's self evaluation of their command competencies were significantly higher than those of women in terms of supervising problem officers and officers with more street experience. Problems in rank-and-file officers accepting supervision from women is not just a cross-gender issue; Brown and Grover (1997) report examples of (American) women being uncomfortable in taking orders from women, preferring a male supervisor.

Deployment

Boni (1998), despite difficulties in the availability of data, undertook an international review of policewomen's deployment patterns and found similar patterns in which women tended to be over represented in routine patrol duties, communications (radio despatch) and support functions and under represented in more specialized duties such as traffic, dog handling and detective investigations. Boni (1998, p. 9) proposes two dimensions associated with differential deployment. They are the continuation of policemen's belief that women are unsuited to certain types of policing tasks which serve to keep women out, and policewomen's attitudes where they self-select out of some and into other specialisms. Boni concludes (p.12) that informal practices, such as discouraging women from applying for specialist appointments, implicit use of quotas and misplaced gallantry in overprotecting women, serve to reinforce differential deployment of women officers. Moreover, unenthusiastic commitment to equal-opportunity philosophies, weak implementation of policy, and resistance to flexible employment practices further undermine gender integration (HMIC 1993, 1996; Prenzler and Wimshurst 1997; Brown 1997). Boni (1998, p. 23) concludes:

> On the brighter side, women's representation is continuing to increase to a point where some evidence suggests, women are close to being represented equally in some previously exclusive male domains. Furthermore, although women tend to be over represented in other domains, this may simply reflect personal preferences. Nevertheless, the reasons that women prefer certain roles may reflect negatively on management practices (e.g. needing to escape from negative male attitudes and competition, lack of personal satisfaction, aspirations and ambition)... The gloomier picture is that formal EEO legislation and policies seem to have been insufficient to ensure the integration of women into all spheres of policing.

There are relatively few studies that look at the preferences police officers exercise in terms of the area of policing they wish to work in. Martin (1989a, p. 7) suggests that the bias of women in support departments is, in part, a function of the push-pull thesis: 'the desire of women to escape patrolmen's harassment, to use the clerical or administrative skills that they may possess and to obtain daytime hours more compatible with family life than rotating shifts of patrol assignment'.

However, Holdaway and Parker (1998) observe from their study of officers from a Northern English police force that women were as likely as men to be interested in evidence gathering and marginally more interested in making arrests and interviewing suspects. In one of the few performance comparisons conducted on British officers, Brown and Neville (1996) found there to be differences in the arrest rates of men and women officers with the latter more likely to arrest shoplifters and the former more likely to arrest burglars. Brown and Neville (1996) discuss possible reasons for this in terms of gender-specific deployments. Holdaway and Parker (1998) find there are still attitudinal biases amongst policemen that preserve gender differences in terms of perceptions about women's supposed lack of career commitment and physical strength. Results indicate that men were perceived more likely to be assertive, emotionally stable, to show leadership and have the ability to control violent situations. Women were more likely to be thought considerate, to prevent conflict and exercise self control. Brown, Maidment and Bull (1992) had shown that, for the most part, men and women police officers did not differ in self rating in terms of these attributes, but that sergeants thought they differed in that certain attributes were more likely to be found in either men or women. As a consequence, this was shown to influence deployment decisions. As a result, argue Brown, Maidment and Bull (1992), women may be directed into low-frequency, high-intensity deployments such as rape offences that decrease their operational exposure to a wider range of high-frequency, less intensive tasks. Coffey, Brown and Savage (1992) show that women officers often cited limited experience as an inhibitor to applying for specialist appointments such as traffic or detective units. Holdaway and Parker (1998) also found that women were more likely than men to indicate that their lack of experience deterred them from applying for specialist posts but men and women were equally likely to be interested in the same type of work. Holdaway and Parker (1998) report behaviours by women officers in the force that they researched that support the token dynamics discussed earlier: women act more aggressively, play down gender, work twice as hard, constantly feel they have to prove themselves, worry about mistakes and feel obliged to say 'yes' to work requests; women were more likely than men to report being worried about their work performance especially as rank increased. Brown (1998), in a comparison of women officers serving in the US, UK and Australia, reports that they were most likely to engage in adaptation strategies (where they worked harder or sought to gain additional qualifications) compared with men: a result also found by Maniloff (1998) when looking at the experiences of French policewomen.

Brown, Maidment and Bull (1992), Scott (1997) and Holdaway and Parker (1997) find that women officers are more likely to feel unsupported by or positively blocked by male supervisors especially for ranks higher than sergeants. Holdaway's and Parker's explanation is as follows: senior officers are concerned about the minority status on women's ability to manage male subordinates. This sets up a negative spiral in that the reasons why women do not apply for promotion or specialist appointments are the same as the reasons why they think they are unsuccessful. However, they also make the important point that not all differences are a function of the exertion of male control and that women themselves play a part in the different treatment but are unable to explain why.

In her formulation of identity theory, Breakwell (1979) argues that individuals need to secure a satisfying social identity and will act to achieve this largely through knowledge of and emotional significance attached to group membership. For women, socialization into normative gender group membership emphasizes their responsibilities as mothers and homemakers (ethic of care), whilst for men, it is their responsibilities as breadwinners (Frone, Russell and Barnes 1996). Breakwell (1986, p. 71) argues that by adopting atypical employment, women fail to conform to gender expectations in job choice and this leads to suspicions about their femininity. If she happens to have a partner and/or children, she is even more vulnerable and may be castigated as being a bad wife or mother. Within the police service, this logic is rehearsed as follows: children get into trouble because their mothers are not around at home; a policewoman parent is not available to look after their child, therefore she is both an unfit mother and an unfit police officer. This is reminiscent of the deprofessionalizing/defeminizing rhetoric discussed in the previous chapter. A version of the unfit policewoman is neatly illustrated by the following example from an Australian policewoman:

I have had some interesting experiences in policing since becoming a mother. After returning to part time work after the birth of my first child, I went to an incident where a young chap had gone berserk and smashed up his parents' house and seriously assaulted his father. I and a junior male officer stepped forward to take hold of him, at which he began struggling. Other police arrived and a well built young officer said, "Wendy, I'll take him, maneuvered me out the way to physically get him into the back of the police truck. The other officers all left, taking the offender back to the police station. A senior male constable remarked to me after we had got the chap into the back of the truck, "I didn't think you did that sort of thing anymore". I was puzzled for a while and then realized that he was referring to my status as a mother. However, it didn't stop them from leaving me with the victims, organizing medical care, obtaining of statements, charging the offender and all the other cleaning up that mothers are so good at. (Austin 1996)

The unfit mother attitude can be found in the research by Holdaway and Parker (1998) who report that a third of policemen agreed with the statements 'on the average, a woman who stays at home all the time with her children is a better mother than a woman who works outside the home at least half the time' (compared to 6 per cent of women) 'women officers who leave to have children should not expect a job waiting for them if they come back to work' (compared to 8 per cent of women) and 19 per cent of men agreed with the statement that 'women officers who want to be mothers should not expect a serious career' (compared to 4 per cent of women).

Thus, law enforcement falls squarely into the masculine domain with societal stereotypes of manliness mapping directly onto the attributions of being a good cop (Berg and Budnick 1986). For women, policing is sexually atypical employment. In order to retain as much femininity as the regimen allows (Brewer 1991a), women officers may seek to map onto the 'emotional labour' of police work which operates to draw them into the marginalized social services policing (Fielding and Fielding 1992, p. 206). Fielding (1988, p. 159) found a grudging acceptance of women probationers by their fellow officers as training proceeded. 'The WPC [woman police constable] belongs to the feminine world of emotion, sensitivity and academic niceties like paperwork, the PC is the man of action and strength' (p. 163).

Impact of women on the police culture

New agendas

Heidensohn (1996b, p. 6) notes that:

> Police agendas are set by several sources in democracies, not least the police themselves and draw on both technical and political sources. A notable feature of several Western democratic societies in recent times is the way in which new priorities have been set for police organisations. New approaches such as community or problem oriented policing have been tried out, as have more domestic

or softer priorities...In some instances this has clearly led to the advance of women as they have been recruited to new tasks or units or deployed to improve their agency's image.

These new approaches owe much to developments in Britain where the Conservative Government of Margaret Thatcher began a revolution in the public sector by introducing private sector management techniques. Further initiatives included the citizen's charter where public sector organizations were obliged to set clear commitments for their levels of service provision. Cobut (1994) describes a similar kind of cultural audit that took place within the Belgium police that would be easily recognized in Britain. Koch (1998, p. 178) describes 'Neues Steuerungsmodell', a German version of new public sector management, in which the police 'are beginning to accept business-like managerialism...improved customer orientation and better motivation of personnel'.

The implications of this have been to manage by agreed objectives, decentralize resource responsibility, output orientation and conduct internal staff surveys of opinion as well as surveys of customer satisfaction with police services. Given the exchange of police methods and philosophies that are presently taking place between Western and Eastern Europe, it is unsurprising to find these trends discernible in the newly emerging democratized police services of the former Eastern Bloc. Similarly the expertize on offer to former British colonial countries to support developments in policing look remarkably like these models too (Marnoch, personal communication). Moore (1994, p. 191) discusses managerial changes in Australian policing in line with other 'Anglophone industrialised democracies' that seek better recruitment and training, organizational restructuring and creation of greater accountability. Given this kind of globalization of change, we might expect to see some changes in attitudes towards and use of women officers. Belmans (1994) indicates the particular role for women newly entered in Belgium police forces: 'The Police Judiciare has little experience with women in the combating of organised crime though we may state that these few women have enormous motivation...a different perspective on this sort of work, which can have an enriching and a refreshing effect.'

However, in an earlier discussion (Heidensohn 1992) the point is made that women were often dragooned into the police to offset some crisis of confidence, as 'a desperate remedy' to solve problems in recruitment, offset scandals or moral panics and calm concerns about rises in crime. Thus women's fortunes within policing seem to have been advanced by some external circumstances rather than change resulting from their presence in policing. On the one hand, arguments, both historical and contemporary, have been presented that women's increasing representation in policing is likely to have a beneficial reforming effect (Worden 1993; Brown 1997; Miller 1998). This position can be linked to notions drawn from Carol Gilligan's work which theorized gender differences in moral values. Gilligan proposed that men and women have different ethical styles in which men's approach is characterized by the *logic of justice* whereby rights, autonomy and impartiality are valued. Women are supposed to be more in tune with social responsibility and affective connections resulting in an *ethic of care* approach. Thus, their analysis of problems as well as their preferred solutions are likely to be different. As such, the presence of women is predicted to have a transformative effect on operational style, organizational management and probity of police conduct. Silvestri (1998, p. 153) reviews the outcome of a transformational agenda should women be represented in greater numbers and at higher rank in the police: increased focus on crimes of violence perpetrated against women and children; change in emphasis from proactive to reactive policing; improved probity of conduct; precipitating other shifts in attitudes such as those towards ethnic minorities and homosexuals. On the other hand, Worden (1993, p. 229) questions the assumptions underpinning the transformational thesis. She finds ample evidence to show that women in policing experience a cool if not hostile reception from male colleagues. However, Worden questions the basis of the inference that treatment of women police officers by male colleagues, *per se*, means that women see their job differently to men. Worden concludes 'one must therefore remain skeptical (albeit not disbelieving) about the claims that women bring to their beats a distinctive perspective on policing'.

Heidensohn (1986, p. 293) rehearses arguments for feminine and masculine values pervading the dispensing of justice. The 'Portia' model of justice is one in which the norm is male, values are rational and individualistic, and the concept of justice invoked is legal and procedural. An alternative is the 'Persephone' model in which the norm is female, based on values of the personal and caring in which the concept of justice is based on responsibility and co-operation. Masters and Smith (1998, p. 20) suggest that, as a consequence of the application of Persephone approaches, various informal resolutionary procedures such as reintegrative shaming, mediation and reparation have been adopted around the globe. Thus, insights from a feminist ethic of care have arguably had an impact on the dispensing of justice.

Marshall (1998, p. 80) constructed a gender balance index (GBI) based on the proportion of women in criminal justice agencies (including the police) and related this to rate of reporting violence against women and degree of female empowerment in societies. There was no indication that as female representation in the criminal justice system increases, women victims were any more likely to report violence. However, there was a positive, if weak, statistical relationship between GBI and the female share of earned income and percentage rate of female economic activity. In other words, as women become economically more active, they are more likely to be represented within criminal justice agencies, but numbers of women in these agencies were unrelated to the likelihood of women reporting violent victimization.

Operational style

Criticisms of male police officers' undue use of force and the crises of confidence induced by rising crime figures and specific crime problems related to youth and drug subcultures and apparent impotence of either police or politicians to combat these have led to the new police agenda discussed by Heidensohn mentioned above. In Britain, the maintenance of order has always been a focus for the police alongside a role to protect and reassure. Brown and Waters (1996) argue that these two roles oscillate with one or the other being at the leading edge. Thus in the 1970s and early 1980s, public disorder of major proportions occurred in several urban centres – Bristol, Brixton and Merseyside. It was during this period that the police [men] donned their new protective gear, riot shields, flame retardant overalls and NATO helmets to combat public disorder. Women, by and large, were initially excluded from such 'tooling up'. Campbell's (1993, p. 3) analysis of a later outbreak of riotous behaviour, on some of Britain's more disadvantaged housing estates, observed there was little difference between the 'incendiary young bucks and the boys in blue' in their love of excitement and the chase of high-performance cars. This resonates with arguments advanced by Fielding (1994, p. 47) that violent confrontation is justified by 'Levitical notions of punishment'. The canteen is the place where war stories are recounted, and warrant is granted for self-serving rule bending and breaking. Similar analyses prevail in Australia (Prenzler 1992; Chan 1996); the United States (Martin 1979, 1989a) Netherlands (Eikenaar 1993) and Poland (Trzcinska 1996).

Crises in legitimacy of policing have arisen in the United States particularly after the Rodney King affair. Heidensohn (1992, p. 202) writes of the 'dramatic testimony to the disastrous effects of machismo'... where the Christopher Commission reported on the beating of Rodney King and found a confrontational style in which women's presence within the force was not only resented but considered a hindrance to a (desirable) macho culture. Australia has had a number of Commissions of Inquiries into police corruption and their excessive use of force. Wimshurst (1995, p. 279) reports that the Queensland Police were found to be inward-looking and defensive spawning a 'blue curtain of silence which supported the emergence of corruption and mismanagement'. Scandals in Europe, notably Belgium and Eire, involved sexual abuse cases. Fielding notes the crisis in legitimacy for policing was located in decline in support for the contract of policing by consent, collapse of police evidence in high profile trials, documentaries on the dispensation of street justice, decline in crime clear-up and the coming to light of corruption amongst serving police officers. Anxious to restore the loss of public confidence in Britain's police, some of the newly appointed chief constables increasingly emphasized the caring nature of the police's contemporary role. Many police forces dropped the word 'force' and assumed a 'service' orientation (Becker and Stephens 1994). These trends were formalized into the ACPO Quality of Service initiative whose aims were laid out in a document entitled 'Setting the Standards for Policing: Meeting Community Expectations' in which equal opportunities is afforded a central place (Holdaway 1996). The document explicitly stated there to be a direct correlation between attitudes within the organization to minority officers (gender and race) and officers' attitudes to members of the public. This resulted in a rediscovery of community service and the reinvention of community policing. Such a cycle of thinking has occurred in other police jurisdictions within Europe (Brown 1997), the United States (Miller 1998) and Australia (Finnane 1990).

Perhaps the most noteworthy example of this re-think was a police strategy that came to be known as 'zero tolerance'. Dennis (1997, p. 3) outlines this as deriving from the simple philosophy of 'nipping things in the bud'. In other words, not letting anti-social elements believe they are in charge. In addition, there are zero tolerance polices with low-intensity, good-natured, tolerant control. The logical extension of this is that petty crime reduction indirectly creates an environment less hospitable to serious criminals. An early version of this was 'strategy five' developed by the New York Police Department entitled 'reclaiming public spaces' conceived by the mayor and police chief (Giuliani and Bratton 1994). The starting point was not a discussion drawn from ethic of care model of justice but rather Wilson and Kelling's 'broken window' thesis based on the rational logic that unaddressed disorder is a sign that no one cares and invites both further disorder and more serious crime. This cycle could be interrupted by first engaging in an analysis of the decline in quality of life sufficient to cause a migration from the city. This pinpointed persistent anti-social activities of drunks, panhandlers, street peddlers, and vagrants which resulted in people abandoning their use of parks and public transport only to lock themselves behind closed doors. Strategy five was intended 'to reduce the level of disorder in the city [in order to] undercut the ground on which more serious crime seem possible and even permissible' (Giuliani and Bratton 1994, p. 5). This was to be achieved by working systematically and assertively in partnership with public and private agencies to combat these social nuisance offences, the theory being that this increases a sense of civic pride and induces citizen responsibility which in turn are likely to impact crime rates. Bratton (1997, p. 33) describes this approach as a shift from the professional era epitomised by O.W. Wilson to a policing philosophy based on work by J.Q Wilson.

How do women fare in this new era of community policing? Interestingly, in Bratton's (1997) own description of the strategy, there is no explicit mention of a role for policewomen. The language adopted used terms like 're-engineering' 'strategic crime fighting'; the strategy was managed by 'comstat' twice weekly meetings in the Headquarters 'War Room' which involved '(1) accurate and timely information (2) rapid, focused deployment (3) effective tactics (4) relentless follow-up and assessment' (Bratton 1997, p. 38). By such rhetoric, New York and other American cities such as Chicago, sought to 'win the hearts and minds of police officers who will be carrying out these new policies' Miller (1998, p. 101). Miller argues that these more community-based policies present a difficulty for police organizations. Demarcation of women into community-focused and victim-centred policing was not only the norm historically but also served to emphasize the differences between policemen and policewomen to the detriment of the latter. Thus Miller (1998, p. 103) states 'men were celebrated as paragon police officers: brave, suspicious, aloof, objective, physically intimidating, as well as willing users of force. Women's femininity, by contrast, stressed . . . partiality, subjectivity, gentleness, conciliation and a focus for affective connections.' Community policing not only rejects the male policing model but positively embraces feminine qualities as ideal traits for the neighbourhood police officer. This dilemma is graphically expressed by Roger Graef (1990, pp. 2–3) with respect to British policing 'asking street hardened coppers, whose self respect is defined by the approval of their peers, to take on the morality and ethos of community policing is like expecting them to police in drag'.

One way to elevate previously disdained feminine qualities to a more desirable status is through an adroit piece of public relations by marketing community initiatives as 'zero tolerance' thus giving an acceptable macho tag for a soft community option. Moreover, as Miller (1998, p. 108) observes: 'Until the police reconcile the contra-dictions that arise when feminine traits are appropriated by masculine experts, dismissing women officers' behaviour as timid or natural while commending men's behaviour, the acceptance of community policing will remain merely symbolic.' Whilst the British version may eschew the 'heavy' handedness of the tactical implications of zero tolerance (Pollard 1997, p. 48) one Metropolitan police commander not only borrowed the language but melded it into the Met's intelligence-led policing (Griffiths 1997, p. 128). A feature article in Metropolitan Police's newspaper *The Job* (May 1998, issue 6) describes the transformation in the policing of the Churchill Gardens housing estate with the caption 'the Churchill spirit' con-juring up macho imagery of regeneration in desperate times.

The thrust of the British Government's police reforms, especially those enacted through the Police and Magistrates Courts Act 1994, still identifies crime fighting as the key policing activity (Loveday 1996). The Metropolitan Police's Operations – Bumblebee and Eagle Eye – epitomize these centrally driven directives by targeting burglary and street robbery and emphasize arrests as a key perform-ance indicator. As shown by Brown and Neville (1996): 'arrest is a significant performance indicator that both fulfills the competitive nature of the informal culture and satisfies the Audit Commission and Home Office for tangible results.'

Fielding (1994, p. 54) argues that whilst women certainly perform patrol duties, the time they have to do this may be impeded by their engagement in 'emotional labour' either easing social relationships within the station or supporting women and child victims of crime. It follows, suggests Fielding, that it is still hard for women to collect a portfolio of 'good' arrests and achieve the all-important street credibility in the eyes of their male colleagues. It is this apparent failure to achieve success in prized activity of the informal culture that helps perpetuate the belief that women are less effective police officers. Brown and Neville (1996, p. 300) propose that efforts to reform the working practices of the British police through an accountable 'performance' culture simply map on to many of the competitive and masculinized feature of the informal rule bending and breaking of the canteen/locker room culture. Holdaway (1996, p. 81) vividly describes the potency of the rank-and-file informal culture in which excitement and action predominate, subverting the more discerning approach to police work advocated by police managers, for example, the ability to influence operational police styles away from masculine stereotype which, according to Fielding (1994, p. 55), 'is unlikely to find much room for expression within the social service aspects of policing'.

Another example of a realignment in policing style can be exemplified by changes in the policing of crimes of violence against women. Jones, Newburn and Smith (1994) note the increasing interest within the criminal justice system in the problems of women and violence. This, they argue, is due in part to awareness-raising by the feminist movement; public attention provoked by the media; and the results of research. The police in Britain responded by developing operational procedures that included the setting up of dedicated units staffed by specially trained (usually women) officers. Jones, Newburn and Smith (1994) examined four British police forces. All had specialist units to deal with rape, sexual assault and domestic violence. The units were mostly staffed by women although usually line managed by a male Detective Inspector. Jones, Newburn and Smith (1994) report improved efforts in training officers to deal with rape cases but less improvement for domestic violence. Often, the role of women officers in the units was not properly appreciated. They concluded (p. 131): 'although it appeared that some improvements in the ways that police deal with rape victims had been made, doubts were raised about the extent to which this new enlightened approach had extended'.

On balance, forces' policy changes had been greater in the area of rape rather than domestic violence. Furthermore (p. 155), 'policy statements at the top of the organization do not necessarily reflect what is happening on the ground'. In responding to the proposition stated by Heidensohn earlier that these new initiatives advance the scope for policewomen, Walklate (1995, p. 197) suggests this to be somewhat optimistic:

> how can policewomen take seriously, and encourage their predominantly male colleagues to take seriously, an area of work historically labeled as 'rubbish' work...[this tension] foregrounds a potential area of contradiction between espoused policy commitments, especially with respect to equal opportunities and what appears to be...deployment of policewomen in...low status work.

Lees (1997, p. 184) notes that whilst police officers seem committed to making victim-sensitive policies work, at another level 'it is important to realise that old attitudes die hard and also the policies are subject to conflicting pressures'. A similar ambivalence is reported to characterize attitudes towards rape in Australia. Nixon (1992, p. 38) suggests: 'There has always been a contradiction between how police construct their role as protectors generally and how they deal with victims of rape...police attitudes have often reflected stereotypes that allowed them to dismiss a complaint of rape as being provoked and therefore deserved, or never having happened anyway'. Nixon goes on to argue that police reform, better education policies and more open attitudes have led to changes in commonly held attitudes. An initial response officer (IRO) scheme was introduced in New South Wales Police in 1987 but male officers found difficulty in a balance that might see an innocent man convicted of rape rather than a victim's attacker go unpunished. The greater harm was perceived to have been inflicted on the former.

In 1994 a survey of University students in Oxford revealed that fewer than ten percent report a rape to the police (Jordon, Mallindine and Glasner 1994). Research from Finland indicates that fewer than ten percent of serious assaults in domestic relationships are brought to the attention of the police (Heiskanen and Piispa 1998). Research reports police failure to act in cases of domestic violence. McVeigh (1994) examined sexual violence in Northern

Ireland. Reported rates are the lowest within the United Kingdom. McVeigh concludes that these results are indicative of under reporting rather than non-offending. Moreover, a link is made between the police's apparent lack of response and the wider environment of patriarchal and sexist structures that exist within Northern Ireland which is compounded for officers of the RUC by their being routinely armed. This legitimation of the means of preserving law and order, argues McVeigh, is also in part responsible for male police officers overlooking the realities of sex crime in the population, and sexual harassment of their own women officers. Domestic violence, rape and child abuse are becoming emergent issues for Eastern European States in transition (*Guardian*, 7 February 1998) with transfer of expertize from West to East to police these offences (Burtenshaw, personal communication).

Probity

A number of key incidents serve to highlight the breakdown of police community relations. Oftentimes, the focus is on race as in the much publicized beating of Rodney King by Los Angeles Police Department officers, a force which, Pollard (*Police Review* 29 October 1993) caustically observed, had achieved the fastest response times and highest detection rates of all US forces. In Australia, a documentary film 'Cop it sweet' made of the New South Wales Police caused a furore over the racist, sexist and profane language and attitudes exhibited by officers (Chan 1997). In Britain, the investigation of the Metropolitan Police's handling of the Stephen Lawrence murder resulted in perhaps the most significant inquiry into racism within the British police service.

As a legacy of the supposed moral superiority of women in general and the civilizing effects policewomen are supposed to exert on the wayward, Lersch (1998, p. 70) suggests that women officers are more likely to have a calming effect on police–public encounters and be more effective in diffusing potentially volatile situations. Lersch undertook an analysis of the rate at which citizens in the US complained of misconduct such as the excessive use of force, discourtesy, dereliction of duty or other inappropriate behaviour such as using position for some personal gain. Only 5 per cent of all complaints were levelled at women officers. Lersch (1998, p. 78) concludes that although the research study was not conclusive, nevertheless women officers appear to engage in fewer behaviours likely to bring complaints from the public. Other studies have suggested that women officers do engage in more ethical behaviours (Miller and Braswell 1992). They suggest that these differences may arise because male officers do not accept them – hence they are not incorporated into the male 'brotherhood' of officers. Waugh, Ede and Alley (1998) found from a study of Australian police that indeed women were less likely to have a complaint made by the public but there were no consistent gender differences in terms of perceptions about the seriousness of breaches of officer conduct. Neither were women officers any more likely to report a fellow officer for misconduct than their male counterparts. The authors conclude that the policewomen in their study were no more virtuous than their male colleagues. The crises brought about by the collapse of the Soviet Bloc meant that Eastern European Police forces had to reinvent themselves. In Poland, this was characterized by 'czyste rece' or 'clean hands' in which officials need to be seen to be untainted by their association with the previous regime. Thus the rhetoric for policewomen in previously communist police forces is anti-corruption. A St Petersburg woman officer Raisa Kurochkina states: 'It does not matter in my work that I am a woman, but I think we are more responsible, disciplined and humane... I never take bribes. I was brought up in a Siberian village and I know the price of labour. I value honesty' (*St Petersburg Times*, 21–27 March 1995).

Conclusions

• There is a time gap between jurisdictions in terms of the efforts made to develop equal opportunities policies and implement initiatives such as mentoring, affirmative action and grievance procedures. Generally speaking, there has been very little evaluation of these initiatives in terms of the achievement of objectives or their cost effectiveness. There is some evidence to suggest a closing of the career aspiration gap between men and women but Heidensohn's (1992) somewhat pessimistic conclusion about an overall improvement in the structural representation of women at higher ranks within police organizations remains valid.

• There have been concerted attempts to implement policies that are more victim centred and community focused (which are said to represent feminine aspects of policing). These have more to do with other organizational and managerial changes than equal opportunities *per se*. Again, there appears to be a developmental lag in police jurisdictions in terms of a recognition of the problems of violence against women. There is as yet no evidence to support the proposition that having more women in law enforcement agencies increases the rate at which women report violent victimization.

- The numbers of policewomen continue to rise, albeit slowly, and there are increases in recruitment of women and the implementation of career breaks and part-time working; yet the overall percentage of policewomen still has to reach the critical mass said to be sufficient to inhibit stereotyping of gender minorities. There is a dearth of research that unpacks the impact of numbers. What is available suggests that there is not a simple linear relationship between numbers and the levels of discriminatory behaviour. The duties, geographic location and administrative position of women officers appear to play a role.

- The small percentage of senior women makes them susceptible to 'token' dynamics whereby they find themselves visible and singled out for special attention in ways that their male colleagues are not. There is some research available that testifies to the presence of token dynamics but very little research is available that examines whether women's supervisory style is different to that of male supervisors and what impact this may have on the supervised.

- Despite some advances, as women entered into more operational spheres, there has been evidence of a resurgence of rhetoric deployed to counter the application of equal opportunities within the police that resonates with historic lines of argument discussed in the preceding chapter. A letter published in *Police Review* (11 July 1997) stated:

> As far as discrimination goes, you will never completely eradicate it – the nature of mankind is too complex for that. The good Lord in his wisdom made male and female different. Most people accept that. The male is traditionally the provider and it is feasible that this could be a reason why there are not so many women who reach high rank in the service. It is not anything to do with discrimination, but rather the desire many women have to curtail careers to concentrate on a role as mother and wife.

- Studies have shown similar reasons given by women officers for their apparent lack of enthusiasm for applying for specialist duties or promotion: lack of experience, belief that their applications are blocked, lack of support from senior officers. Women are shown to respond positively to schemes to encourage their careers, but as yet few of these schemes have been formally monitored.

• The number of cases being brought to industrial tribunals is increasing. The financial expense and cost to the force's reputation are high as is the personal cost of undertaking litigation. More officers are winning cases, for example, in Finland (*ENP Newsletter*, February 1994), England (*Police Review*, 22 May 1998).

• There is some divergence emerging in the research literature in terms of the presence and persistence of discriminatory behaviour. Martin (1996, p. 526), for example, suggests that in the force she studied, men and women thought that promotion and career opportunities were equally accessible to both male and female officers. Holdaway and Parker (1998) document internal and external constraints that continue to play upon the employment experiences of women officers in the force they studied. These differences may be due in part to methodological considerations: Martin's study was based on small-scale qualitative interviews whilst Holdaway and Parker undertook a large-scale quantitative survey. It may also be attributable to the differences in force policy and commitment of chief officers. There may be differences in scale – Martin's research was conducted in a provincial rural force whilst Holdaway and Parker examined a large metropolitan force. Comparative studies controlling for some of these dimensions – size of force, energy of implementation of equality policies, qualitative and quantitative research methodologies – may help to unravel the differences in the research conclusions.

• There would appear to be differences in perceptions of some policewomen in terms of progress and their judgement that circumstances have improved (Martin 1996) and those that believe there is still embedded sexism, some of which is more insidious because it is now less overt (HMIC 1996).

• Further evidence of globalization is present, particularly within Europe, in terms of EU-wide equality legislation and other Community directives, as well as direct exchanges of policing practice and management techniques between Eastern and Western Europe in which victim focus places an emphasis on women officers.

5

Filling in the Picture: The Empirical Details

Introduction

Research into the histories, roles and experiences of policewomen have tended to concentrate on single countries (for example, Wales: Jones 1986; India: Aleem 1989, Natarajan 1996; England: Young 1991, Martin 1980, Australia: Prenzler 1994, Wimshurst 1995; United States: Hunt 1990, Martin and Jurik 1996). Findings are difficult to compare because of the varying dates and methodologies of the studies. Chapter 3 testifies to the universal resistance to women's entry into policing, whilst the previous chapter illustrates the widespread occurrence of sexual harassment, differential deployment and blocked career progression. Cross-cultural research into women police, by and large, has been confined to US/UK comparisons (Heidensohn 1992; McKenzie 1993). Only more recently have analyses extended to include other countries (France, England and Wales: Dene 1992; Europe: Brown 1997).

We have previously rehearsed the explanations for this lack of research activity, to which we add difficulties in negotiating access to research populations of police officers (for discussion of this problem, see Jones and Newburn 1994; Horn 1996; and Walker 1997). Difficulties of access are further exacerbated if the topic of the research is especially sensitive and whose findings may lead to adverse publicity (Lees 1997, pp. 178–9) or the sample being accessed is inherently low in numbers as in the case of policewomen (Wertsch 1998, p. 26).

Approach to the present research

We outlined in broad terms our solution to these research problems and indicated three axes of our analytical approach for comparing the experiences of policewomen. Heidensohn (1992) had previously drawn attention to the importance of grounding the evolution of policewomen's roles historically. This provided our first axis – structural dimensions of time and numbers. Heidensohn (1992) developed a series of conceptual tools with which to examine the experiences of policewomen from the United States and United Kingdom and which Brown (1997) had extended in a wider cross-cultural comparison. These concepts, together with psychological processes, become our second axis. The third axis is provided by the typology of police organizations, discussed in detail in Chapter 2. Thus equipped, we examined some constants and contrasts – one task of comparative analysis (Mawby 1990, p. 4). Previously, in Chapter 3, we described the discourses used historically to thwart women's progression within policing through the maintenance of a rhetoric that women are inherently unsuitable for the task of policing. This allowed us to examine the basis for differential deployment and sexual harassment of women officers. We also examined the organizational structure of police, in particular the impact of gender ratios in Chapter 4. Having completed the historical analyses and conducted a literature review of available research on the contemporary position of women officers, we now present a snapshot of the current position of presently serving policewomen in order to (a) compare with the historical data and (b) extend the analysis cross-culturally. We also had a number of more specific questions:

1. What is the impact of different gender ratios in terms of discriminatory experiences and coping adaptations?
2. Does a sense of self-efficacy overcome the impacts of the informal police culture?
3. What are the coping strategies adopted by policewomen?
4. What empirical validity is available for our proposed taxonomy of police organization?

We also wanted to flesh out the bones of the quantitative analyses with qualitative accounts, to illustrate some of structural processes with the muscle of individual experience. (Details of the qualitative data gathering and analyses are presented in the following chapter.)

Measures

We designed a questionnaire that was available in English and French. This sought demographic and occupational details of the officer: age, marital status, number of children, length of service, country served in, rank, role in the police. We also asked how many men and women served in their particular unit/shift. From this, we calculated the gender ratio. Officers were asked how accepted they felt by both male and female officers, whether or not they experienced discrimination in deployment, promotion, training or overtime opportunities. There was a specific question about their experience of sexual harassment from fellow officers, men or women. We asked how they coped in the police environment and what support strategies they used. Finally, we adopted the short version of a self efficacy scale used by Breakwell (1992). There was space on the questionnaire for officers to offer any further comments. (A full version of the questionnaire is provided in Appendix 2.)

Sample

Several different sampling strategies were employed:

- The research departments of the Garda Siochana and Royal Ulster Constabulary were approached and requested to distribute a survey to women officers in order that a comparative data base could be established from which findings were to be presented to the 1996 IAWP/ENP conference. One hundred questionnaires were distributed by the RUC and 50 by the Gardai. Response rates were 62 (62 per cent) and 38 (76 per cent) respectively.
- The British Association of Women Police agreed to send a copy of the questionnaire with conference details. Membership drew from officers serving in forces in both England and Wales. Seventy completed questionnaires were returned (58 per cent response rate).
- The European Network of Policewomen (ENP) agreed to distribute a copy of the questionnaire (in English and French) with their newsletter with an appeal for recipients to provide comparative data for the 1996 IAWP/ENP Conference. This yielded 117 completed questionnaires.

• Questionnaires were distributed to two conferences of police-women held under the auspices of ENP in Hungary and Poland in December 1995 and April 1996 which yielded 38 completed questionnaires from women officers serving in a variety of Eastern European countries.

• In preparation for the 1996 conference, delegates at the 1995 IAWP Milwaukee conference were approached to complete the questionnaire. This yielded 186 responses from serving American policewomen, and 43 from those serving in Canada.

• In 1996, Australia held the first conference of Australasian police women. Officers were approached through a magazine distributed to policewomen seeking their participation in the study and 206 completed questionnaires were returned by Australian officers, 7 from New Zealand.

• Two senior women serving in African police forces, Malawi and Botswana, were also approached to assist in data collection. They distributed questionnaires and 26 from Malawi and 12 from Botswana returned usable completed questionnaires.

Analyses

Data from the questionnaires were coded in a conventional way and subjected to analyses by the Statistical Package for the Social Sciences (SPSS). When presenting analyses of the total data set some statistical procedures were conducted. Correlations and analysis of variance are duly reported. Because of the disparate nature of the sample and the small sample sizes in the cases of particular countries, we ventured some caveats in the interpretation of results. We also made use of multivariate statistical procedures drawn from the Guttman–Lingoes program (Hammond 1990). We used Multiple Scalogram Analysis (MSA). The method of MSA requires a matrix to be constructed – in our case, countries which make up the rows – and the columns comprise the variables of interest, – in our case, degree of acceptance by policemen, amount of discrimination and sexual harassment experienced, and ratio of men to women in each jurisdiction. The data were recorded as a profile for each country in terms of a dichotomous score, indicating whether that particular country's policewomen experienced above or below average on each of the variables. MSA then represents the similarities between profiles by location of points in a scatterplot in which profiles that are similar will be positioned close together whilst those that are dissimilar will be positioned further apart. Interpretation is made in terms of our *a priori* typology of police organization: transitional, gendarmes, cops and colonial histories. In other words, countries will be represented as points in the plot and lines of partition are drawn to see if identifiable regions can 'capture' countries that we think belong in one of our proposed types. If this can be done the empirical data thus provides 'correspondence' (verification) of the conceptual scheme (Borg 1981). A second Guttman analytical procedure is also employed: partial order scalogram analysis (POSA) which is an extension of the Guttman scale. This is where endorsement of one item predicts the endorsement of another, for example, if an individual indicates they have a Ph.D. it is very likely they have an undergraduate degree and gained some kind of advanced school-leaving certificate. However, holding of a first degree does not predict that the person also has a doctorate. Thus the prediction is directional. It is thus possible to construct a set of symmetric profiles, that is, from having no qualifications (no school certificates, no first degree, no Ph.D. represented as 000) to a set of specified academic achievements gathered in a particular order (school certificate, first degree, Ph.D. represented as 111). The set 000, 001, 011, 111 reflects all combinations for a perfect Guttman scale. POSA allows for the possibility of non-symmetrical profiles; in other words, an individual having a school-leaving certificate, no first degree but holding a Ph.D. is given a profile of 101. This procedure is employed to examine how policewomen in our sample make use of coping and support strategies.

Results

Description of the sample

In all, we collected 804 usable questionnaires completed by presently serving policewomen from 35 countries (a full listing with frequencies is given in Appendix 3). A brief overview of the total sample indicates that our modal policewoman is white, thirtysomething, has served an average of 12 years, is likely to be married or living with a partner, has no children, and works as a patrol officer or a detective.

Table 5.1 Descriptive frequencies of the survey sample

Age	N	%
20–30	221	27%
31–40	399	49%
41–50	155	19%
50plus	26	3%
Mean	35 yrs	
Marital status		
single	271	34%
married/with partner	437	54%
divorced	88	11%
Ethnic origin		
white	716	89%
non white	82	11%
Children		
none	469	58%
some at home	295	37%
some not at home	37	5%
Length of service		
1–10 years	350	43%
11–20 years	363	45%
20 years plus	88	11%
Mean	12 yrs	
Rank		
Constable	393	49%
Supervisor	384	48%
Duties[*]		
patrol	280	35%
investigation	224	28%
training	70	9%
administration	183	23%
traffic	24	3%
support	100	12%

[*]   officers were asked to tick their main area of duty, but some ticked more than one hence % do not sum to 100%

Experience of discrimination and sexual harassment

The overall experience of discriminatory behaviour indicates that about a fifth of all women officers in our sample feel that they are unaccepted by a few/some of their male colleagues whereas they feel unaccepted by only about 5 per cent of their women colleagues. They are most likely to have been discriminated against in terms of differential deployment and over three-quarters will have experienced some form of sexual harassment from male officers.

From the open-ended comments given by our respondents, some qualitative examples indicate the kinds of experiences policewomen have had. The following comments are from women serving in forces we designated as 'cops':

I was sexually assaulted at work and have spent over one and a half years of attacks from within and outside our agency.

I have had personal experiences of sexual harassment and found that until proceedings got to the internal enquiry stage I was treated badly and made to feel that I was lying and was treated as an offender not as a victim. However, when the inquiry proved that I was not the first female officer this sergeant had touched, the Department could not do enough to keep me happy.

I feel that men's decisions are met with more seriousness. Senior men have more influence than senior women. Women are still seen as sex objects that should not be in the job.

Table 5.2   Overall frequency of discriminatory exposure

Acceptance	by men	by women
by all	14% (115)	49% (379)
most	58% (470)	28% (305)
some	16% (132)	5% (44)
few	7% (57)	2% (11)
none	0.5% (4)	0.1% (1)
Mean	*2.1*	*1.5*
Experienced discrimination		
deployment		52% (420)
training		31% (253)
promotion		28% (222)
overtime		17% (134)
Mean		*1.2*
Sexual harassment		
never	23% (183)	76% (613)
rarely	33% (263)	10% (840)
sometimes	34% (271)	5% (39)
often	7% (58)	0.1% (1)
Mean	*2.26*	*1.2*

An officer from a force with a former-colonial tradition writes:

> The degree of discrimination is very high against women. Unfortunately there are
> no female activists who can voice their concerns so that equal opportunities
> attitudes. There are only a handful of male officers who understand the subject
> of gender sensitization while the majority do not recognise female officers as full
> equal participants prevail [*sic*].

Being married, and/or pregnant can also present difficulties for
women officers as some of our respondents testify. Police organizations do not seem to be able to cope with women in dual roles as
either wives or mothers whilst fellow officers seem resentful at what
appear to be concessions made to women colleagues. Women serving as 'cops' stated:

> As a single parent I experienced great difficulties being a policewoman and mother.
> Where I work, my situation as a single parent is of no concern to my male colleagues
> and this causes me great stress and a difficult living situation for me and my child.

> Although the Garda have an equal opportunities policy it does not appear to be
> working very well i.e. women on maternity leave are still not being informed of
> positions becoming vacant or applications for promotion being forwarded.

> I recently got married to a fellow serving member. I was transferred over 90 miles
> from my matrimonial home. This was appealed and turned down, appealed again
> at transfers appeal board and turned down again. How am I to have a marriage
> (which won't end in divorce) as my authorities seem to be doing everything they
> can to separate us?

Similar sentiments were expressed by an officer serving in a force
having a former-colonial history:

> As a result of taking maternity leave my position as a traffic officer in education
> was filled. On my return from 11 months leave I was given the position as driver
> testing officer and enquiries officer. I do not get any job satisfaction from my
> present position and have been doing this monotonous job now for 2 years.

Coping and support

Women officers use a range of support and coping mechanisms and
many use a combination of strategies.

   In terms of their adapting to the police occupational culture and
demands of their work, women officers are least likely to use the
resources of the union/staff associations or formal organizational

Table 5.3 Overall frequency of use of support and coping strategies

Coping	N	%
union	86	
being aggressive	161	11%
complain to a senior officer	191	20%
say nothing	366	24%
joking	411	45%
being assertive	425	51%
Mean	*2.1*	53%
Support strategies		
union/staff association	94	11%
senior woman officer	199	25%
female colleague	251	31%
equal-opportunity policies	256	32%
male colleague	375	47%
senior male officer	418	52%
work harder	526	65%
gain extra skills	532	66%
Mean	*3.0*	

Table 5.4 Overall frequencies of profiles: support (bold) and coping (italics) strategies with average discrimination scores

Strategy profiles				Self-efficacy	Harassment	Discrimination	Acceptance*
self	**peers**	**organization**					
			% using				
1	**1**	**1**	**(25%)**	**18.28**	**2.42**	**1.46**	**2.15**
1	**1**	**0**	**(34%)**	**18.42**	**2.36**	**1.49**	**2.30**
1	**0**	**0**	**(13%)**	**18.67**	**2.32**	**1.39**	**2.30**
0	**0**	**0**	**(10%)**	**18.10**	**1.94**	**0.71**	**2.01**
1	*1*	*1*	*(6%)*	*18.59*	*2.30*	*2.35*	*2.51*
1	*1*	*0*	*(15%)*	*18.46*	*2.75*	*1.83*	*2.32*
1	*0*	*0*	*(60%)*	*18.36*	*2.29*	*1.15*	*2.16*
0	*0*	*0*	*(12%)*	*18.48*	*1.15*	*0.38*	*1.89*

* lower scores mean greater acceptance.

equal-opportunity policies but rather rely on their own resources by working harder or gaining additional qualifications. Women cope by using humour and being assertive. As explained above, we can construct profiles that illustrate that women are likely to use a range of strategies. Thus, by categorizing both coping and support strategies into those that are derived from self effort, peers and organizational sources (senior officer, union) we can form a perfect Guttman scale to account for 82 per cent of our sample in terms of support strategies and 93 per cent of a sample for the coping strategies. None of these measures are statistically significantly different although there are some trends observable. First, there is a more even spread in use of support strategies with the highest proportion, a third, engaging self-help and help from peers. Coping, on the other hand, is dominated by employment of strategies based on one's own resources. It is unlikely that officers placed sole reliance on peers for support (7 per cent) or coping (0.5 per cent), and few place sole reliance on the organization for support, (2 per cent) or coping (2 per cent) (see Appendix 4 for full set of frequencies). Some examples from the open-ended comments to the questionnaire illustrate policewomen's experiences. A women cop writes:

> I presently have good support in the command that I am presently in. But I have experienced great difficulty in the past with being accepted on equal terms. I worked in the homicide squad for a number of years and experienced great isolation and discrimination from certain members. This greatly influenced my decision to look elsewhere for promotion. It worked. I got promoted and my contemporaries didn't.

A woman from a gendarmerie comments:

> My colleagues in the same rank see me as a threat because they think because I'm a woman with a university degree I'll get better position/higher rank, so I don't show my capabilities and qualities.

And a woman officer from a force having a former-colonial history observed:

> Being one of the first policewomen when senior officers did not know how to handle us I had to put up with a number of frustrating circumstances. To be accepted in a higher position I had to work extra hard to prove myself capable of doing as well as my male colleagues or even better than some of them.

Interestingly, highest self-efficacy is associated with officers who invoke only themselves as their sources of support but self-generated coping strategies is associated with lowest self-efficacy. Those who use the greatest range of support strategies (profile 111) are also likely to report highest levels of harassment; those using no strategies (000) report lowest levels of harassment, discrimination and highest levels of acceptance. This pattern is repeated for use of coping strategies. These results suggest that greater activation of support and coping strategies is associated with higher levels of reported discrimination and harassment.

Table 5.5 summarizes the correlations between average number of coping strategies employed, self-efficacy and gender ratio with indices of acceptance, discrimination and sexual harassment. Self-efficacy appears unrelated to any of the discrimination effects, but the greater the discrimination and harassment and not being accepted by male officers, the more coping strategies are used. The present analyses cannot help us in terms of directionality. In other words, if women are exposed to greater levels of discriminatory behaviour, do they marshall a greater range of adaptive strategies or are women, whose repertoires of strategies are greater, either attracting more discrimination or more likely to interpret behaviours as harassing? Brooks and Perot (1991) provide an indication of directionality from their study of university faculty members and students. In this study, women who scored more highly on feminist ideology were more likely to perceive behaviour as offensive. Perceived offensiveness was a significant predictor of preparedness to report behaviour as harassing. So perhaps, officers who have more developed adaptive strategies are more likely to experience behaviours as offensive, hence the trend for higher reporting. So we might have a threshold effect here? In other words, exposure rates may be similar, but it is factors associated with women's levels of awareness and preparedness to name behaviours as offensive that might account for individual differences in reporting rates.

Table 5.5 Correlations of coping and self-efficacy with indices of discrimination

	Coping	Discrim	Ratio	Non-accept	Sexual harassment
Discrimination	$.46^{**}$				
Gender ratio	$-.004$	$-.06$			
Non-acceptance	$.23^{**}$	$.35^{**}$	$-.04$		
Sexual harassment	$.52^{**}$	$.44^{**}$	$-.01$	$.30^{**}$	
Self-efficacy	$.06$	$.01$	$.03$	$.04$	$.03$

$^{**}p < 001.$

Numbers

Using Kanter's (1977) topological divisions to define groups by gender ratio, the following analyses are presented to try and establish some systematic relationships between numbers of women to men and presence of discrimination and harassment. None of these analyses were statistically significant suggesting there is no linear relationship between aspects of discrimination and gender ratio as predicted by a strict application of Kanter's thesis.

The optimum percentage appears to be 35 per cent where there is a clear diminution of harassment and discrimination and greater acceptance. However, the impact of numbers is rather more complex than suggested by a strict application of the Kanter thesis. Women cops noted:

> I have told you that there is equality among male and female officers ... but if you look at the numbers of women police in our force (male 169/female 8) you can imagine how equal we really are ... (more equal in principle than in practice).

> To be the first female officer in a small local police of a small town for five years was the hardest job I have ever done. There was no one to turn to. My colleagues (males) tried to help when they had to, but I missed a female and someone I could put trust in. Sometimes I got wrong answers to my questions or no answers at all.

> Our police department is very male dominated and we few female officers have a constant struggle against the ingrained police culture.

Figure 5.1 Percentage of policewomen to men and levels of discrimination and acceptance

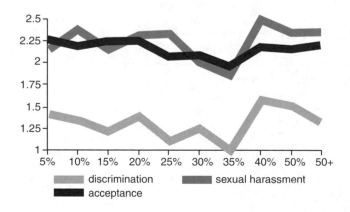

An African policewoman expressed a similar sentiment thus:

> Serving in the police is very good. The only problem is that officers (males) do not want to listen to ideas being introduced or given by a female. They try and ignore female officers and if you are not brave you can shrink. So female officers need to stand on their feet and show the male officers that we are capable of doing the job.

If the ratios of women to men are calculated in terms of Kanter's categories: dominants (N = 53) majority (N = 17); gender balance (N = 29); minority (N = 139); token (N = 448), then, results suggest that as women gain in numbers, the rate at which they are accepted by other women increases until women become dominants in which case there appears to be a drop in the percentage of acceptance. Thus, there does not necessarily appear to be a solidarity of acceptance of women by women when women are in either the minority or dominant group as the following quotations from policewomen serving in the Anglo-American tradition of cops illustrate:

> My recent promotion to sergeant has left me baffled. Prior to this I was supported and encouraged by both co-workers and bosses. Now, working in a different area, I find little if any support from my male co-workers. I find that the females in my command would rather let a male tell them what to do. I'm puzzled why there is so little support for females from each other in this job.

> I've worked my way through the hard way. My only possible mentor retired before I could benefit from her. Other females have sabotaged my efforts to succeed.

> I have recently given birth to my son. When I was pregnant I was immediately transferred to a non operational police area. I am an investigator working shift work and was assigned to a dayshift research position. The area was not my expertise. Consequently I lost a considerable amount of money not having shift penalties. I also served a position in another suburban detective branch before I advised my police department that I was pregnant. My new officer in charge (a woman) told me that I should never have got the position and told me that the other staff were angry I was on parental leave. I am entitled to 12 months. I have taken 3 month parental leave and 6 weeks annual leave and 5 weeks long service leave. My officer in charge questioned my intentions on returning to work because I have taken so much leave.

The possible reasons for this may well tap into different dynamics. When women are the dominant gender, they may well be competing with each other for prestige or status. When in the minority, they may be competing for survival. The picture of men's acceptance in different balanced groups indicates less acceptance as women come to dominate the gender balance. The next analysis examined indices of discrimination under conditions of different gender ratios.

Figure 5.2 Percentage of discrimination in differently
proportioned groups

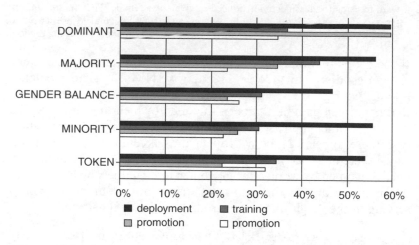

Figure 5.3 Percentage of harassment in differently proportioned
groups

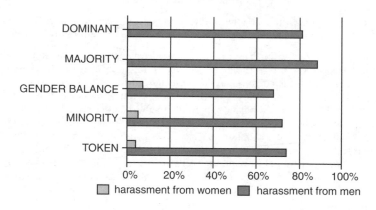

The general pattern of discrimination, as shown in Figure 5.2, associated with gender ratio of working groups reveals a U-shaped relationship. In other words, as the ratio places women in the minority there is a relatively high level of discrimination and harassment. Movement towards gender balance is associated with a trend for less discriminatory behaviour to be practiced but as the gender ratio becomes dominated by women, there is again an

Figure 5.4 Percentage use of support strategies in differently proportioned groups

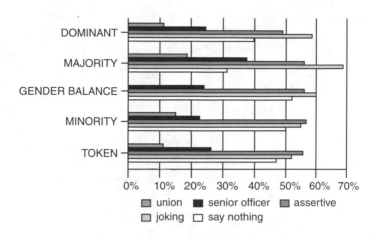

increase in the amount of reported discriminatory behaviour. Sexual harassment from men appears least when there is a gender balance but actually increases when women are in the majority. However, there appears to be a different relationship between gender ratio and sexual harassment experienced from other women, shown in Figure 5.3. Here, although considerably less overall, nonetheless there appears to be a modest increase in rate of reporting of sexual harassment by women on women, associated with higher ratios of women in the police work environment. As with the previous analyses, use by women of support strategies does not appear to be related to gender ratio in a simple linear fashion.

By and large, there is an overall trend suggesting that discrimination and harassment tend to be least when there is a measure of gender balance. If women are in the minority or majority there appears to be an increase in the discriminatory behaviour. It may well be that there are different dynamics at work. When women are in the minority, the token dynamics cited by Kanter and found in studies of token policewomen (Ott 1989; Wertsch 1998) operate. However, when men are in the minority, it may well be that they increase their discriminatory behaviour as a way to restore their sense of control and preserve their access to organizational benefits.

Figure 5.5   Time of entry and levels of discrimination and coping

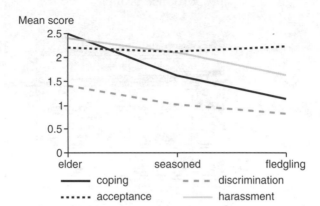

Time

In Chapter 1 we discussed the use of time, that is, the original dates of women's entry within police jurisdictions, as a comparative dimension. Three broad categories were defined for the purposes of the present analysis: World War I to World War II = elders (479); Post-War to the 1970s = seasoned (73); Post-1970s = fledgling (60). Four aspects were examined: the average number of coping strategies deployed (population mean = 2.1); the levels of acceptance by policemen (population mean = 2.1); the average levels of discrimination experienced (population mean = 1.2), and the average levels of sexual harassment reported to occur from policemen (population mean = 2.1).

The analysis shows that, in general, it appears not to matter how long policewomen have served in the various jurisdictions: the general levels of acceptance of police officers remain constant. However, there is a statistically significant trend showing that the more fledgling police organizations, in terms of women's involvement in policing, have lower levels of discrimination and harassment reported and fewer coping strategies employed. A more detailed breakdown of these results by individual items from the questionnaire and their statistical details are provided in the Appendix 4. In summary, the pattern is the strongest and most consistent of all the quantitative analyses in the linear association between the time dimension and levels of discriminatory and harassing treatment: the longer woman have been employed in a jurisdiction, the greater their level of complaint and the more likely they are to make use of coping and support mechanisms. The time variable overlaps somewhat, although not completely, with the cross-cultural classification in that many of the European gendarmeries only recently recruited women officers and so are to be found in the fledgling category. However, other European forces have employed women since or before World War I and will be found in the other time bands. Rival hypotheses to explain these findings are: that the fledgling forces are more progressive and women have less to complain about; the tolerance threshold idea, whereby women newly entered into policing are less likely to challenge behaviour and tolerate the *status quo*; the maturity of equality legislation whereby women have the confidence to challenge hitherto taken-for-granted behaviours. Given the military traditions of fledgling forces and the glacial pace of attitudinal change, indeed even some evidence of regressive thinking charted in the previous chapter, we are more inclined to the tolerance threshold thesis. In other words, we find it a more persuasive argument that women in police organizations with older traditions are more likely to define behaviour as unacceptable rather than assume men are less likely to engage in unacceptable behaviour in jurisdictions only recently admitting women.

Cross-cultural comparisons

A second dimension of our comparative analysis is the cross-cultural one. We constructed a typology, outlined in Chapter 2, defining police organizations as coming from the Anglo-American 'cops'; European models of gendarmes and transitionals and those hailing from countries with colonial histories. We first wanted to establish empirical verification of this typology. This was undertaken by application of a multivariate analysis MSA. Where countries in our sample had sufficient numbers, the average levels at which women officers were accepted, average gender ratio and the average rate at which women from those jurisdictions reported harassment and discrimination were calculated and country profiles constructed. The analysis presented in Figure 5.6 is the resulting MSA plot. This demonstrates partial support for our typology. Albeit with only two transitional jurisdictions, Poland and Hungary

Figure 5.6   MSA plot showing distribution of countries by policing
typology

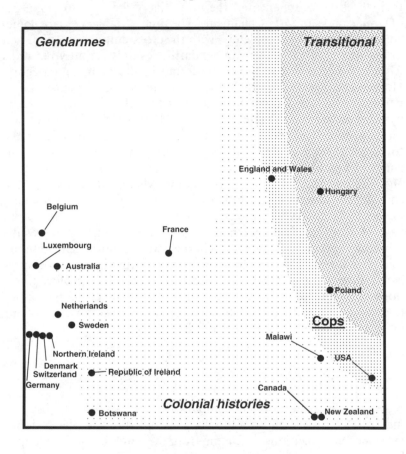

having sufficient respondents for this analysis, a line of partition can
be drawn that shows them occupying a distinct region at the right of
the plot. We can also draw a further partition capturing a region in
which England and Wales and the United States appear as 'the
cops'. We could not include Australia, which appeared in our
original specification of cops; rather, this is captured in the region
in which jurisdictions having colonial histories appear. There seems
to be two distinct types of colonial jurisdictions: Canada, New
Zealand and Malawi forming one cluster and Botswana, Republic
of Ireland and Australia another. Finally, we have a region in which

Table 5.6 Cross-cultural comparison of levels of reported discrimination (classification is based on the MSA results)

	Promotion	Deployment	Training	Overtime	Sexual harassment (often/ sometimes)
Cops	40%	65%	47%	23%	56%
Colonial	25%	57%	29%	17%	39%
Gendarmes	18%	32%	22%	8%	31%
Transitionals	53%	55%	35%	62%	34%

European forces, the gendarmes, appear. Interestingly, Northern Ireland's Royal Ulster Constabulary is present in this region of the plot, suggesting women officers in this force share similar experiences with women officers from other European military forces.

When we examine specific areas of discrimination, then we can demonstrate differential aspects of discrimination. Women cops appear to experience greatest discrimination in terms of deployment opportunities and, more than in other types of policing, face limitations on training opportunities and also are the most likely to report experiencing sexual harassment. However, women from the transitional forces are the most likely to report facing promotion blockage and restricted overtime opportunities. Generally speaking, women serving in Western continental forces, the gendarmes, are the least likely to report discriminatory experiences. Women serving in forces having a colonial history are less likely to report discrimination than the cops or transitionals but more likely than the gendarmes.

Summary

- These results suggest that time as a comparative dimension proved to be the clearest differentiation of policewomen's experiences in that those from the elder forces (earliest to admit women) were almost twice as likely to report being discriminated against and to experience sexual harassment than those from fledgling forces only recently recruiting women. Respondents from the seasoned forces recruiting women post-World War II consistently reported intermediate rates of discrimination and sexual harassment at levels between the seasoned and fledgling forces. We propose there to be differences in the tolerance threshold of women's awareness, labeling of behaviours and preparedness to report these as unacceptable, rather than, necessarily, differential levels of discrimination and harassment.

• Our proposed typology of cops, gendarmes, transitional and colonial history receives partial support. We were unable to verify inclusion of Australia in the Anglo-American type, it appearing empirically to be more similar to jurisdictions having a shared former-colonial history. Similarly, the Royal Ulster Constabulary appeared more closely allied empirically with police forces having gendarme characteristics. Women from the gendarmes were most likely to indicate that they were accepted by male colleagues whilst the women from the transitional former Eastern Bloc were least likely to be accepted. Generally speaking, patterns of discrimination followed the degree of acceptance with women from the gendarmes least likely to indicate that they suffered differential treatment in promotion, deployment overtime or training opportunities. By and large, women from the transitional forces most often reported discrimination. The pattern for sexual harassment was a little different, with officers from the cop tradition most likely to report experiencing sexual harassment, and women from transitional forces and the gendarmes least likely to complain.

• We were unable to support a strict demonstration of a linear relationship between the Kanter gender ratio thesis and rates of discriminatory behaviour as there were no statistically significant results. In general, it did appear that as gender balance was achieved, this was associated with lower levels, although not elimination, of discrimination. Higher levels were reported by women who were in either gender minority or majority working groups. In other words there was a U-shaped relationship. We speculated that different dynamics may be at work in processes that operate against women when they are a token presence compared with men on the one hand, and when men are the token in a work unit of mostly women on the other.

• We wondered if women's sense of self-efficacy might be related to the adaptation to the police working environment. Our results show no statistically significant relationships between self-efficacy and number of coping or support strategies employed. As there are no established norms for self-efficacy it is not possible to comment on the relativity of scores in the present study. There were no differences in self-efficacy scores between the respondents in terms of the countries in which they served. The average score of 26 was higher than the average reported for young people in the study (average 23) by Breakwell (1992). Self-efficacy was not associated with levels of reported discrimination or harassment. This suggests that, irrespective of a policewoman's belief in her capabilities, she is likely to be exposed to differential treatment or sexual harassment which we take to mean that the impacts of the occupational culture are hugely potent and can override an individual's efforts.

• Women tend to use more problem-orientated methods for coping although a significant proportion use emotion-focused coping by joking or avoidance (keeping silent). Browne (1995) explains the apparent passivity and helplessness exhibited by abused women as corresponding to 'antagonistic co-operation'. This is a situation in which the weaker partner develops a strategy to facilitate survival and obtain leniency. Browne argues (p. 240) that battered women's affective, cognitive and behavioural responses are likely to become distorted because of their intense focus on survival. This is akin to rape trauma syndrome in which an acute disorganization occurs after the attack (Mezey and Taylor 1988). Rape victims also invoke denial and avoidance strategies; 'some [victims] experience an almost childlike dependence on their attacker and . . . victims said that they had thanked their attacker after he had let them go, without clearly understanding why they should have done this' (Mezey and Taylor 1988, p. 333). We would argue that in some cases, the police environment creates an abusive relationship where the woman officer experiences something akin to the battered wife and rehearses similar coping responses. Their investment in their career is parallel to the investment in a relationship. The longer time is served, the more difficult it is to admit the abuse and the less likelihood then of leaving. There may be a trigger event that changes the definition of the situation and allows a woman to name the abuse and taken some action.

Through our qualitative analyses, we can explore these issues in some greater detail and it is to this we next turn.

6

Personal Stories: Comparing Careers

Introduction

In this chapter, we focus on the views of a group of officers whom we interviewed during the first truly international conference for policewomen, held in the city of Birmingham in England, in September 1996. While other congresses have drawn delegates from many countries, this one, organized jointly by the International Association of Women Police and the European Network of Policewomen, attracted the widest range from across the world, with only Latin America as an area lacking representation. Because of our interest in gender issues in policing and our work on projects in this field, we were determined to use this event as a unique chance to interview those in attendance. It offered us the opportunity to gain access to an international sample, gathered in one place at the same time; it enabled us to contact women from parts of the globe which were harder for us to reach because of cost and distance; finally, we could add to our sample, subjects from nations and agencies where the low numbers of females employed would have added to the effort and problems in finding and interviewing them.

Planning well ahead and using three additional interviewers, we exceeded our targets. By the close of the conference we had sampled 24 countries and conducted 42 interviews involving 56 individuals. (Some of the interviews were conducted with pairs of officers; two were with deliberately selected groups). Our coverage included officers from four African countries, four Eastern European and three Far Eastern societies, although the USA and the UK were most strongly represented by twelve and nine interviewees respectively. In Appendix 5 we give more details about the

126

interviews, a fuller account, together with a discussion of some of the issues this research raised, can be found in Heidensohn (1997).

The importance of this material for the themes of this book is twofold: in the first place, it provides directly given accounts by policewomen complementing the survey responses which we have already presented. Secondly, we are able to make comparisons with some of the other qualitative studies of the careers of female officers, especially those cited in the comparative chapter above. Most of the material in those accounts was gathered through a mixture of observation and interviews; the latter mainly conducted in a police setting. Using a conference as our base meant that none of the women were on duty (although they appeared in uniform on some occasions during the five days) and thus we could not record their actions and reactions to real policing situations. (At least one law-and-order episode did occur away from the convention centre which a respondent reported to us.)

Almost all the interviews were taped and later transcribed in full; all were conducted in English, the language of the conference, except for one where an interpreter was present and another in which a European language was used. Respondents were asked about their reasons for joining the police, their career history, their experiences as women in a masculine occupation, their judgement about their own and their agency's style of policing and their predictions for the future of policing. We also asked quite detailed questions about their experiences of networking and other forms of liaison and support.

The length and detail of the career histories which we were given varied considerably. Surprisingly, perhaps, two respondents had only about three years service; on the other hand, several others had thirty or more. Interviews took place in different settings in and near the convention centre and this also led to fuller accounts being given in some cases as more time was available. English was not the first language for half the sample, although they spoke it very well and for some, it was the medium through which they had studied or in which some of their work had to be carried out. A particular feature of all the subjects of this part of our study is that, as officers attending a high-profile international training conference for women in policing, they had already developed awareness of some of the issues in which we were interested.

Careers and concepts

As we have outlined above, researchers on the role of women in policing have, since the pathbreaking work of Susan Martin (1980) sought to analyze their topic within distinctive frameworks. Martin herself proposed a continuum of adaptations to the traditional male culture of the occupation from police WOMEN to POLICEwomen. The former were conventionally feminine, while the latter adopted masculine styles of behaviour. Since the women we were interviewing were not on duty it was not practical to try and assess them in these terms. In any case, it is very unlikely that the police WOMAN type will be found in modern law enforcement; rather, they came from the older, separate policewomen's bureaux and departments. Sandra Jones had already noted in a study in Britain: ' "traditional" women who most regretted the demise of the policewomen's department...were more likely to display predominantly police-WOMAN characteristics' (Jones 1986, p. 172).

The other studies which have been based on qualitative data (Brewer 1991b; Lanier 1996) also derive from observational accounts and produce models which do not lend themselves easily to comparison with our material. They are, like Martin's, grounded in a single country and indeed one law enforcement agency, even though Lanier partly draws his taxonomy from Brewer's work. Instead, we have used the framework derived by Heidensohn in her earlier comparative study of US and British officers. There are greater similarities between these two groups of officers in terms of numbers (50 interviewed by Heidensohn (1992)), range of ages, ranks and tasks; moreover, her framework was developed for use in an international comparative study. (And of course, she was involved in both projects). As will become clear, the original set of concepts had some applicability to the lives of the women interviewed in Birmingham, but there were also areas where notable differences appeared. The importance of the historic dimension discussed above became apparent in very striking ways in these interviews. Finally, the conference itself was important as both a formal, training-focused occasion for police officers and *at the same time* a significant ritual occurrence which had certain shared and specific meanings.

For her earlier analysis, Heidensohn developed what she describes as 'a set of soft, pliable concepts which could helpfully be used to focus on aspects of these women's life histories...

basically organizing ideas...[to] be used...analytically to... explore key questions' (1992, p. 117). The concepts (which did not all have the same salience in both countries) are:

- A sense of mission
- Pioneers
- Partners
- Transformation scenes
- Professionalism
- Soft cops
- Female cop culture
- Top cops

How closely did the experiences related by our international group in the 1990s resemble those of the British and US officers in the late 1980s in content and in meaning?

A sense of mission

Policewomen in Britain in the earlier study 'all reported a strong, and often continuing, sense of mission' (Heidensohn 1992, p. 125). This is partly derived from the occupational culture where it is given primacy: 'A central feature of cop culture is a sense of *mission*... policing is not just a job but a way of life with a worthwhile purpose' (Reiner 1986, p. 88). The US officers shared this aim too. In both groups there were examples of women who had struggled to enter law enforcement, showing great determination and, in America, resorting to legal action. Once inside, their dedication had frequently been tested by harsh and challenging conditions, largely imposed upon them by their male colleagues. Some of the 1990s group were similarly drawn to law enforcement:

> I had the clear thought that I could help people and that I might not be able to solve all the problems in the world but for fifteen minutes a day at least solve someone's problems for that day and that I would be helping people (No. 22).

> I wanted to do something that would help other people (No. 49).

Two African American officers stressed their idealistic aspirations:

I went into...law enforcement...you have these ideas when you're young that
you can change the world regardless of what goes on (No. 17).

idealism. I saw some real injustices that I thought I could correct, just wanted to
do something about the injustices that I saw (No. 16).

Most of these officers had been recruited since the watershed of
integration of the male and female branches of policing, which
occurred in the 1970s in Britain and the USA, but at other dates
elsewhere. The battles for entry which some of the earlier sample
reported, which related to fixed quotas for women in Britain, and a
reluctance to hire, retain or promote them in the USA, were largely
absent from these accounts. Nevertheless, one US veteran described
her guileful persistence in obtaining forms for promotion exams and
in encouraging numbers of her women colleagues to take these
exams. A much younger British woman, taken on after integration,
recounted her campaign to gain entry despite apparently not meeting an existing height requirement.

However, there were other, perhaps less noble, ambitions behind
these women's decisions. Several had sought to join a uniformed,
discipline service, such as the military:

my original ambition was to join the army (No. 30).

or another wished to be a naval or airforce pilot (No. 43). Since
women were not then accepted into those services in their countries,
they chose the police. In two other cases, the women had been
working in or with the military when their roles were civilianized
and they became police officers. Family ties were, for some, a factor:

I'm from a family of four or five police officers...so it seemed a natural thing for
me to do (No. 3).

my father had been in the police (No. 9).

although at least one had *defied* her father to enter, while another
had been a hairdresser and felt goaded by a patronizing boyfriend
who was a policeman into applying. Contrasting attractions cited by
some women ranged from variety and excitement:

wanted something that offered more variety (No. 4).

the hustle...the blue light...the boys and the uniform and the cars (No. 40).

Through chance:

> I really became a police officer by accident, because I never really intended to (No. 13).

or:

> curiosity... why not go, try and see if I can do this (No. 10).

to security: ˙

> it was for money! I saw financial stability (No. 15).

> that was the attraction, it was a good salary (No. 47).

as one respondent frankly commented:

> the salary, in combination with it being an appealing job with the uniform and being something... I think that was more the reason why people joined... than any kind of social aspect, but of course many people named it as that on the application form (No. 38).

A notable feature of several of these histories was that they had been recruited during a drive targetted at women, minorities, or both. Here are comments from three African American officers:

> My department was looking for minorities and I kind of doubled up because they were looking for women, and particularly black women (No. 15).

> On mine it was particularly 'We're looking for minorities'. It was during the time that departments had to increase their minorities representation (No. 17).

> When I was hired it was during the latter 1970s, early 1980s and I think a lot of departments in the US at that time were having some sort of drive to include minorities, to include females (No. 16).

In two other jurisdictions a narrower gender ratio improvement had been the target when these women joined in the 1970s:

> at the time government, there was more victims, I think female... women victims and the police didn't know how to handle it... there were just men, they couldn't handle it properly... so it was an outcry from the public (No. 49).

> I came in at a time when they had a recruitment drive to bring up one police-woman per section... there'd only been four women, perhaps 120 guys [then] we were 20 (No. 48).

Inside the police and facing down the culture

Our 1996 conference attenders appear less likely than the earlier sample to report a strong missionary zeal as a factor in their choice of policing as a career. Yet, they were clearly highly motivated to stay in once they had joined. The length of service of the majority was over ten years and only two had been recruited in the 1990s. Several professed a lack of prior awareness of conditions in the police before they entered:

> it has worked out OK but I know I would have thought this person is going to struggle in this job. She is very naive (No. 2).

In common with our survey respondents and the 1980s group, these women faced a huge variety of problems and harassment from their male colleagues. These could be simple rejection:

> off the record, we don't want a woman on the unit (No. 7).

> I will never forget my first night on patrol. It was first shift and I had a lieutenant that had probably twenty years and he just came out and said 'you know, you really need to be at home, this is no place for a woman. I really think you should be at home'. I mean, if I heard that one time, I heard it five times that night (No. 16).

There were numerous reports of difficulties over deployment and promotion:

> I couldn't move up (No. 42).

> as a woman, definitely your credibility took a lot longer to get (No. 9).

> I was trying to have a job with the foreign police ... they took another man ... they would rather have another man (No. 39).

Individuals did vary in their career histories. One officer:

> tried to be riot trained but they wouldn't let me (No. 7).

whereas two others had and indeed recounted the challenges (and the humour) they faced later as Public Order Training Instructors:

> I wore the same uniform as the men ... a flying suit ... huge boots ... body armour ... I'd be standing on the parade square when all the students ... [pre-

dominantly male officers]... would saunter across the parade ground and say 'I hope you've got the oxygen'... 'Well, you are the first aider, aren't you?' And they had such a shock when I started to bark and shout at them and drill them up and down the square... and I said 'I'm *not* the first aider' (No. 4).

being an instructor they were easily able to identify who I was and I had a couple of courses where one individual man who's like determined to take me out, it was like 'I'm not having this woman here, she's going to have to go', and that was quite interesting... it was because I was a female they found that hard to deal with (No. 3).

The majority of our group had been promoted above the basic grade, several also came from agencies which had dual-level entry which they had joined at higher ranks. The proportion with supervisory positions was high and reflected the 'skewed' sample likely to be attending the conference (many delegates, especially from the USA, paid their own fares and expenses). They had thus clearly demonstrated that women could be promoted; nevertheless, this could still be a contentious issue:

when the man gets the job that the man wants to have, it is OK, but if the woman gets the job, it's a big problem, and normal explanations are that she is cute or very pretty, or she has affairs with the chief or something like that (No. 43).

You know the nature of men, they would not want any woman to compete with them (No. 27).

they are afraid of losing their positions and to lose to a woman in the police force... is like dragging down their trousers (No. 34).

This creates a destructive, discouraging atmosphere:

we certainly felt that we had to be twice as good and we were tested more... [they were] waiting to see you fail (No. 9).

if anything, some of them wanted me to fall by the wayside (No. 30).

Traditional macho cop culture has become a much-discussed topic (Waddington 1999; Macpherson 1999) since the publication of *Women in Control?* in 1992. In the histories discussed then, all the women acknowledged the issue of harassment and abuse and some reported gross (and petty) examples of both. Some respondents in the more recent study claimed not to have come across these matters in their organizations:

sexual harassment, grievance, it's like saying you know, what kind of country are we in, we don't understand these concepts because they're not applicable to us but I couldn't tell you the reason why (No. 24).

For the majority, however, episodes such as these were, or had been, characteristic of their careers or those of their colleagues:

> He assaulted me...first I had a relationship with him...that was ended but he wouldn't accept it...it was at my home that he assaulted me, not at work... (No. 37).

> a lot of sexual harassment as well...touching...orally...trying to enforce intercourse...I wasn't raped, I'm lucky (No. 44).

> snide comments and remarks...no end...a lot were...very destructive ...and I was raped by a police officer (No. 2).

There were detailed accounts of how entrenched and supported within the organizational culture such behaviour was:

> You didn't challenge anything...blatant racism and sexism in the classes and the training Sergeants...subjected many students to harassment, both sexual and racial...One sergeant...he'd walk past you in class and grab the top of your thigh to see if you were wearing stockings...a black recruit...was subjected to horrific harassment and comments like 'vagrant and get in the jungle and get your knuckles off the table (No. 3).

When three women all separately reported a male supervisor for sexual assault:

> most of the men were saying 'He's all right, he's a nice bloke, he wouldn't do that' and looking at the women sort of and 'they must be right, he's a nice bloke, he couldn't possibly have done it' (No. 4).

A woman felt doubly victimized:

> I was a victim of sexual harassment after two years. And the policy was then, both the male and and me were transferred. Yeah, that was a bad time... then I wanted to go in another place in the region and wasn't allowed (No. 37).

A considerable repertoire of responses to harassment and abuse was outlined:

> I'm never allowing such a thing...but fortunately I have, I held my ground, I never gave any such idea to them, that they can subdue me, so may be that's the reason why I never saw such a thing (No. 27).

if you just act normal to the men and then the men will act normal with you they [sexual innuendoes] shouldn't be blown up . . . if the women were more assertive in the first place (No. 38).

Staying in and getting on with a career in policing in the face of such incivilities clearly required persistence and commitment. These interviewees were, in more than one sense, the survivors; one described herself as a member of a trio still in the force out of eighteen women who had joined together. Some of the stories related had echoes of the 1980s accounts; indeed many of this sample had years of service which overlapped with the earlier group. All the same, they had had nearly another decade in post and there are some differences in these accounts. Most striking are those analyzed in a later section where the official and collective reactions to the cop culture are recounted.

Pioneers

This concept was prominent in the earlier study because integration (in Britain) and the first women going on patrol (in the USA) were events within fairly recent memory. Some of the British respondents were veterans of the integration process (Heidensohn 1992). Within this second group were also, surprisingly perhaps, several women with long careers in the service, who could look back to the earlier days of policewomen's departments or other separate sections. Their stories chart a lifetime of pioneering steps. One did not resign when she became pregnant with her first child and had to fight with great determination to stay on in the force. By the time her second baby was born:

none of the hierarchy questioned me at all . . . it was just . . . 'Nobody's going to put her off, nobody's going to bully her or threaten her, she's just going to do it' (No. 1).

Subsequently, she broke through a series of barriers and achieved many 'true firsts' as well as changing the culture of her force:

it was a culture shock for my colleagues as well as for me to do this. I think nothing shocks them about me now!

A second officer, from one of the first countries to recruit women began her service in a welfare bureau, but moved on to a series of firsts in much less gender-conventional postings (No. 11). She did not see herself particularly as a pioneer, citing rather her city which she thought had been very progressive in its policies at one time, but had now ceased to be so. These officers will retire in the twenty-first century and the memories of the 'separate sphere' for women in policing will go with them.

Interviewees from nations where women entered policing more recently were more clearly breaking barriers:

> we were the first, we were the pioneers, I was one of the pioneers, there were no other women in the police station, you know, I was the first time lady and that was twenty years ago (No. 49).

They described situations close to the lonesome pioneers in the earlier study:

> I was the only woman there in the...office and in many of the courses I would just be the only woman (No. 26).

A senior officer from a country which falls into the middle bracket in terms of recruitment history had a record of a series of 'first woman to qualify as...' had developed her own approach to handling these situations:

> But it's not because I specifically decided to get out there and say hey I wanna do these things, its just, I was prepared...to try change...There were sort of [barriers] because if you confront anybody with something that hasn't been done before the hardy annuals will get thrown up and say 'I don't know whether you can do that' (No. 48).

The first officer quoted in this section had broken through a barrier by choosing to return after maternity leave. Over a decade later, in a force in another part of the same country, a young detective chose to work right through her pregnancy:

> the attitude changed because being the only woman...in that department, they went from sort of 'you're mad, staying at work when you're pregnant, I wouldn't have my wife at work doing this job', you know, to 'can you go and do some surveillance because nobody will know you're a policewoman because you've got this huge lump' (No. 4).

Many more of the officers in this sample had children than in the previous study; indeed, all of the British women in the earlier group were childless. In that sense, they were pioneers since motherhood and policing had long been deemed to be incompatible.

Some significant changes had happened between the two studies which many of our respondents saw as having a fundamental impact on the old occupational culture. A supervisor approvingly related this episode:

> the younger generation who are reaching more senior positions who are more enlightened and more accepting... what made it for me was when A [senior officer] was at a meeting last week... [and there was talk] about the problem of women who were pregnant and the problems it was causing for management and A summed it up that it was a fact of modern life and it needs proper resource management and that's really all there is to it. Next question (No. 9).

Innovative and open-minded chiefs were cited by several women as key figures in promoting equality for women:

> women officers... can specialise, in fact, the sky's the limit for them in our force. We have a Chief who backs this idea, I have to say, you need a strong Chief (No. 1).

Many insisted that their agencies now had equal-opportunity policies, gave women extra chances (No. 43) or had schemes for part-time work, extended parental leave or other benefits. One considered that life was very comfortable for new recruits:

> Oh, far easier. These women now complain because they don't get enough cramps days OK? When I came along you came to work with the cramps, towel and all included. Now, you know, they even put couches in the rest rooms so if you're having a bad PMS day you can lay down! We didn't have that and don't dare ask! (No. 15).

There were several descriptions of procedures involving discrimination, harassment or other grievance matters. These have clearly become much more common, especially in Britain, and there was considerable familiarity with some of the high profile cases, notably that of Alison Halford. For some, disillusionment had already set in:

> after 1992... I was on a high because I thought we'd achieved a lot and I thought women were unstoppable and had conversations that the Police Service was

changed for good and that we were unstoppable. Then, my experience over the last few years is that the guys have realised that like I did, and they're pulling out all the stops to knock us back (No. 7).

This view was not universal, although another woman who had investigated allegations of sexual assault brought by policewomen against a male colleague was appalled by the treatment of the victims:

> Instead of supporting them and encouraging them to stand up for what the truth was and what had happened they were trying to repress the situation (No. 4).

Despite the widespread adoption of formal policies on equality, cynicism was expressed by some interviewees:

> We have an employment equity policy...I think it's a piece of paper. We all understand, we all feel that it's something that exists but basically is lost through the door once you are in trouble. The person that acts as the Employment Equity Officer is in our Human Resources team, is the most inequitable person anyone has ever seen (No. 22).

A more typical view was:

> I do see the women on my shift being treated in a much better way than women at my time of service were. I do think there has been a fundamental change but I think its so precarious that if we don't keep pushing it, it will slip right back to where it was before (No. 2).

The earlier comparative study yielded responses suggesting that some women felt that they were punished, for being pioneers, with harassment and abuse. Such perceptions seemed to persist in the 1990s:

> [Resistance] is to do with, I think, how the men value themselves. Their self-worth is based on their ability to chase criminals, to catch burglars, to have a punch-up, to do fast driving, and they call that, they claimed for years that that was what policing was about. Suddenly, well not suddenly, but when women became integrated they found that women could do those same things and all of a sudden their self-worth is based on the same criteria as a woman...we're a threat to them personally...rather than professionally (No. 7).

While these officers from 'mature' systems, as far as accepting women is concerned, are either sceptical or cautiously optimistic about equality, those from fledgling services, well-represented in our group, faced a different situation. Frequently they had no equal-opportunity policies in any form (Nos 26 and 33):

> No, if they have then maybe they keep them somewhere where we don't see, we've never seen a policy...and because of that, even if you experience some kind of sexual harassment you don't know how to tackle it because there is no written policy to say if you experience this, you do this (No. 31).

The point of coming to the conference was, for these women, to learn about such matters and to return to their own organizations primed with ideas and action plans.

Pioneering remains, as the role of women in policing enters the second century of its history, a key concept in understanding the phenomenon. While some of the major frontiers have been conquered and the territories subdued, resistance is still strong, especially where developments are at an early stage. Some women report significant improvements which mean that pioneers are supported, even encouraged, and structures and processes are in place to assist them. In mature systems, women pioneers will have less scope, but the wagons may need to form a circle for a while to come.

Partners

Some, especially North American, officers made reference to partnership on patrol issues, but it was not otherwise a main topic for our interviewees. We had of course, no chance to observe them at work either and, with many of them holding supervisory ranks anyway, we were not able to focus on this concept in these case histories.

Transformation scenes

In 1992, Heidensohn explained how she came to consider this key concept in the lives of her subjects. She was seeking to explore how they managed situations of violence and disorder: 'they described events in which they proved themselves in some way, thereby earning the respect of their colleagues...these episodes did effect "a twofold process" the women themselves felt their confidence strengthened and their male colleagues granted them admission, of a kind, to the fraternity of real police' (Heidensohn 1992, p. 142). There was no shortage of such anecdotes in this second study.

Not surprisingly, perhaps, such episodes were focused on the old-fashioned forms of police action, valued in the occupational culture. A woman supervisor was aware that her shift were waiting to test her out until:

> a situation in the town where one of the officers was assaulted and the offender's run off and I chased three and arrested three on foot. And that then, then the shift were completely different towards me, it was like 'Yeah, you've proved yourself now, that you are one of the shift sort of thing, one of the boys, you can get involved' (No. 3).

> We went . . . to a pub fight, and I went in and the whole thing escalated and I just pitched in and made the first arrest and as I was wrestling with this prisoner down the steps and he was thumping me and everything, one of the male members of the shift turned round and said to me 'Welcome to the shift, Serge' (No. 4).

Another interviewee recognized but regretted the necessity for such scenes:

> I did something that I regret doing but I didn't have any other ways – I went out to be one of the boys: I rescued lots of people, I fought with villains, I chased villains, I shouted 'Stop! Police', I went into fights and won some of them and became one of the boys. I regret doing that now but I didn't have any other option (No. 7).

Such initiations were ruefully recalled in the USA too:

> I spent all one night chasing a burglar, bruised my hip up pretty bad and I was working for another Sergeant that night and he turned round 'It'll make a man out of you, you'll be all right' (No. 15).

In her 1992 study, Heidensohn found that some of her subjects reported a series of such scenarios, that each time they moved to a new posting they had to re-enact such mini-dramas in order to be accepted and to be licensed to police (1992, pp. 141–5). In this group, there was much greater variation, partly related to 'the time line' of female entry, in accounts of acceptance into the cop culture. A supervisor from one force at that stage described a position where policewomen undertook *both* old-style duties *and* integrated duties:

> the role that women are supposed to [do]...[is] the duty of women police to look after juvenile offenders... to help young children... to deal with female offenders, that's what is here, written down, it's written and then after they can be deployed on other things (No. 26).

The consequences for her were that she was left out:

> sometimes I thought really I wouldn't make it...I could not be sure exactly what they...I couldn't be with them, drink with them, go out with them.

At the other end of the spectrum were women who had been much more proactive about their own careers, often taking extra courses, additional training or other outside validation in order to engineer acceptance and advancement. This supervisor contrasted changes in her department in recruitment and policing policies:

> when I first started I didn't have the physical attributes of a lot of the bigger guys; at one time, in the 1960's and 1970's in our force we hired huge policemen, who had, this is gonna come back and haunt me I'm sure, had small brains but could beat the crap out of anybody that needed to have... the law enforced upon them... I picked up skills or I enhanced my own skills...I had to if I was gonna survive there, I had to prove myself somewhere else, plus I wasn't too shy about getting into any fight (No. 23).

Among the 1996 group were officers who had benefitted from changes in the organization of policing other than the development of equal-opportunity policies. There were notable developments of specialization, especially the growth of specialized units in larger forces and/or requirements for technical specialists – scene of crime, fingerprint, fraud and so on – within smaller forces. One had escaped a uniform posting into a prestige unit with a different ethos:

> in the department...they are kind, they are very correct and they're very civilized and yes, we're all friends, all of us are friends (No. 35, senior supervisor in a national force).

A member of a much smaller department had become an accomplished specialist in a highly technical area where she had gained both local and wider recognition and this had turned the reactions she received around:

I actually don't have the problem on patrol that I had in patrol services and the reason is that for a woman... I'm in a highly respected job, very highly respected, and that's because I'm an expert and there are some patrol services now come across asking for information from me and I find that because now I have the support and expertize I operate on a different level. I'm not just a woman police officer doing her job for a man... so I'm not competing for that position (No. 22).

In contrast, there were officers who felt that they were stuck in untenable positions where their superiors were seeking to 'retransform' them – either to discourage them out of the service or deflect particular campaigns:

I'm in records and all I do pretty much is shuffle papers to make sure things are in numerical order... they're building a case against me for being incompetent, derelict in my duty, insubordinate so that they can demote me and create a position (No. 13).

Less extreme versions of this involved long-serving officers resigned to no, or slow promotion, and often involved lack of acceptance within the occupational culture. Strikingly, several of these examples came from North America, whereas the stories of strategic moves which transformed policewomen's lives and careers were all from mature European systems. However, a very important note of caution about our conference sample needs to be entered here. Most of the North American officers had paid their own way to the conference, often taking annual leave in order to be there. This is their normal practice. Delegates from Europe and the rest of the world were much more likely to have been officially selected and sponsored by their agencies. It is thus very likely that they were more successful in conventional career terms, and more acceptable to superiors than the self-selected group. Very few women attended from Germany; this was said to be due to cutbacks in public expenditure taking place at the time.

There was still evidence then of the part that transformation scenes played in achieving acceptance into the occupational culture for some respondents. But this was only one route; their impact wore off and for others there were alternatives, such as moves into sections where less macho cultures flourished. For women in fledgling systems, there was a need to rely on the formal command and control hierarchy and to search for ways to find acceptance and combat harassment.

Professionalism

From the very earliest days of women's entry into policing, there was a stress on professionalism, an emphasis on its key components of education, training and discipline (Carrier 1988). Even where, as in Britain, the pioneer policewomen were volunteers, they wore uniforms and set up and ran their own training schools (Allen 1925). This thread still runs through many of the accounts of late twentieth century policewomen. One senior woman from a fledgling state described numerous tribulations in a career in which she had achieved a great deal:

> I think that I was the best, the best in my headquarters. I was a specialist . . . many people come to me about many things because my name was famous (No. 47).

In other systems, there were very similar reports to those in the earlier study of women seeking to exceed male norms in order to prove themselves:

> you have to train very hard physically yourself so that you will perform and almost go, not be one of the lads, but you won't be beaten . . . I look at the effort I put in for that training, far more than the men, because I wanted to do it and because I wanted them to say 'well, she can do it, there's no problem she can do it' (No. 3).

One very senior officer described her approach as being 'super professional' and acknowledged that she was accepted by her (male) peers:

> they say . . . we expect you to be the professional that we know you are and we are, and have loads of confidence in yourself (No. 1).

On the whole, the women in this survey were less likely to cite professionalism in the same way as the earlier group had. However, they did quote their own further and higher education (often undertaken at their own expense) or their on-the-job training and recognition or accreditation as specialists. What they did mention was that the organization of policing was in itself becoming more professional and bureaucratic, with more formal requirements of recruits, greater emphasis on rules, transparency and accountability. There was, in this respect, stress on how women fared well under this scheme because of its objectivity.

Soft cops

This term was originally used to indicate that the early menu
of tasks for female policing included the 'traditional' areas of
children, juveniles and disturbed people. Certainly, some
officers recognized this pre- and post-integration distinction. It
was, not surprisingly, women from the 'fledgling' states who
were most likely to describe their work as being in the traditional
way.

Female cop culture

There were notable differences between the two studies on this
measure. There were numerous listings of links with other women
officers from the fairly simple:

> I've been a mentor for younger officers who came into the Police Force, and
> informally, I'm a mentor, together with another woman, for the other females
> who come in (No. 37).

through descriptions of the founding of informal networks:

> we have our own network organization in–I was at this seminar ... and a lot of
> women were ... and there it all started. We thought it was so fun, sitting, we've
> got a lot of information and education and so on during these days, but most fun
> was the evenings when we were out walking and so on. Of course we talked and
> talked (No. 35).

The Birmingham Conference, the site and source of these interviews, was itself jointly sponsored by the two international bodies
whose aims include the promotion of networking. Thus we were
able to observe, and interview, developments in the formation of
women's networks at three different stages. First, officers from
agencies with low percentages of women had come to Birmingham
to learn about networking, equal opportunities and how to change
their own organization. One had set up a local association of
women police and despite opposition from her chief, was going
ahead with seminars and a dinner. One woman asked the interviewer how long the IAWP and ENP had been in existence. She also
commented that informal networks and support systems were now
being organized in her country with other female criminal justice

professionals (No. 26). Another in this 'fledgling' category described a wider feminist group in her country:

> this is an organization...women who come together to discuss how we can be self-supporting. How we can look after our businesses. How we can go about getting things done and apart from that how we women can develop relationships with other women without necessarily involving men (No. 30).

At the next level were relationships formed during the conference. Two officers from a state with few and recent female recruits were planning, while at the conference, how they might host a similar event at home, link with other women in their region and develop international links. They asked the interviewer how they might go about presenting papers and how they could apply to do this. Another pair from the same force were using the conference to develop their links:

> this is my first introduction to the networks and everything else...we've sat down, we've been opposite ends of the area...and yet we're both going through exactly the same things...we've never stopped talking. A bit like therapy this is! (No. 4).

She and her colleague agreed that they would remain in contact and regretted that no formal forum existed for them to meet.

Finally, there were conference veterans who had attended IAWP events regularly for many years (this was only the fourth ENP conference and the first held jointly with the IAWP). For them, it offered opportunities to create or renew ties with other policewomen. One group had begun by founding a local net-work:

> We're members of the same organization. She [another interviewee] was one of the founders. It was really helpful because had it not been for [her] over my ten years I probably would have killed my partner, shot the Chief, who knows? (No. 17).

Her colleague described the value and nature of their links:

> organizations like this, like I can talk to her or she can call me from—either one, and you can call me from—and you might have a problem that's common to us all and I've been on it twenty years...and we can sort of help her go through something in her department that we've already jumped over the hurdle (No. 21).

Of course, once again an important caveat needs to be stressed: this conference was designed to attract attenders who wished to bond and liaise with their female colleagues. Women averse or indifferent to such events and purposes may be unlikely to come to them. Our group may not be very typical. Nevertheless, we did speak to women disillusioned with the concept of sisterhood! Of a close colleague one said:

> she don't reciprocate the give and take ... she is difficult in that she does not wish to see anyone succeed around her ... she doesn't encourage you, she speaks down ... she distances herself (No. 22).

Others also spoke in negative terms about some of their female fellow officers:

> women ... can be quite bitchy (No. 8).

> female colleagues were very envious (at her advancement) and they were very angry with me (No. 36).

> [a woman] won't help you ... [she] wants you to experience everything she did however difficult that was (No. 44).

Heidensohn had remarked in her 1992 book that female cop culture, manifested in groups, links and magazines was more significant in the USA than in Britain. By the time that book was published, the 1992 ENP Conference had been held at Bramshill, an event which one of the interviewees described as the high point of her career. Networking, some of it officially supported as in Sweden, for example, has developed very considerably. The aim of the ENP is to extend its role in Europe, while the Australasian Council of Policewomen pursues similar goals in the Pacific region.

Top cops

On the first day of the Birmingham Conference, Pauline Clare, Britain's first woman Chief Constable had joined other speakers on a panel to discuss breaking through the glass ceiling. That event had considerable symbolic significance. Certainly, members of the various associations present believed that there were now more women in senior posts in policing:

Yeah, we have...more higher ranking women now. My immediate boss...is a female. My Deputy Chief is a female, so God doesn't stand a chance of sexual discrimination any more, not in my chain of command (No. 15).

A veteran of many IAWP conferences observed that each year the numbers present in higher ranks increased.

For the most part, only mature systems with long histories of recruiting women are likely to have them in senior positions. Several of our respondents could claim that like Chief Constable Clare, they were the first to reach their rank in their own country or agency. Several described vividly the hazards of high rank – isolation, for instance:

this conference has always been my time to come with other women because when I was the only Sergeant, when I was the only woman Commander you never have any peers. So this was my yearly journey, my Mecca to get rejuvenated and that meant you could fight for another year (No. 21).

On the other hand, a very senior and experienced woman described herself as fully accepted and observed with humour that:

I'm a fully fledged member of the Command elite, if you like (No. 1).

She relied on links developed as much with her male colleagues as with her female ones, and considered her key mentor to be a man.

She, like several of the interviewees with higher ranks, commented at length on management and gender topics. Gender differences in management styles were mentioned by some respondents – one said she consulted on decisions where men imposed their will. The value of supportive chiefs was stressed by many respondents. One who had excellent relationships with her own staff was appalled by the poor quality of management and said she 'could not have a conversation with them' (No. 2).

Conclusion

In her original study, the first such international comparison of policewomen's careers, Heidensohn concluded that it was possible to analyze careers in Britain and the USA within the same framework. Many similarities could be observed, though differences were notable on two dimensions – pioneers and the female cop culture.

The picture with the latter group is more complex, but there are some key common concepts, even though there is considerable variance and even contradiction within some categories. The most striking change in the decade between the two projects was the development of networking among policewomen, especially in Europe and, in a less advanced way, Australasia.

7

Conclusions

In this last chapter, we try to summarize the main discussion we have presented so far, highlighting two sides of our central theme: gender and policing. We contrast these two aspects of our theme by calling them gender and policing and policing and gender. By *gender and policing* we mean questions to do with the entry of women into policing and their employment and role in law enforcement, its history and development in different countries. *Policing and gender*, on the other hand, is the headline for the opposite but parallel, side of this story: the ways in which the history of policing women has been distinctive, with women coming into policing in order to control and protect their own sex. Then we consider some of the wider issues raised by our study, both the ones we have tried to examine and those that we think are worth further exploration. Finally, we suggest some of the implications of this work for policy and for research.

Gender and policing

Perhaps the most interesting feature of women's participation in policing is the way in which it was envisaged and depicted long before any policewomen were actually recruited or deployed. This, as we show, is highly symbolic not only for the pre-entry period when campaigns – first to install prison or police matrons to guard female offenders, later to recruit policewomen – were mounted, but subsequently when key themes of a popular discourse about women, or more properly, *femininity* in a masculine occupation were presented and mocked half-a-century before there was any actual embodiment of what they caricatured. As policewomen became established, their images changed while they still remained subject to crude gender stereotypes: either exaggerated or

149

oversexualized or butch and terrifying. Of course, male officers were also often depicted in stereotyped ways during much of the twentieth century especially as P.C. Plod or his colleagues.

The significance of such portrayals in caricature reflects, we believe, concerns about the changing roles of women in society and especially reactions to the ways in which groups of women were getting more fully involved in public life during the nineteenth century and the early years of the twentieth century. A policewomen's movement developed across the world – or certainly in Britain, the USA, Australia and many European countries – during this period. It was not an entirely separate phenomenon; its roots were in first-wave feminism and the associations formed and run largely by women which aimed to engage with social control through moral and welfare reform. Many of the members of these groups were educated and from the middle class, but they also made very effective liaisons with men in influential positions – from bishops to M.Ps – and organizations such as trades unions as well as some working-class women. However, their aims were often to bring order and discipline to the lives of other women, especially where it had public impact. In both Britain and Australia, exceptional wartime conditions are often cited as the catalyst for recruiting the first policewomen; we believe the evidence shows that these were the opportune moments seized by the enthusiasts of the movement to achieve goals they had planned for some time.

While this may be a contentious view, it is nevertheless worth exploring further why, at broadly the same epoch, so many different women and their associates focused on the same solution for central social issues. The answer, in part, is that while there were similar developments at about the same time in different places, they were not totally separate. Indeed, another near key feature linking this early era is the web of international links between movements. Both organizations and individuals liaised across the globe, exchanging ideas and information and mutual support. Often, key charismatic figures, such as Nancy Astor played crucial roles in supporting the introduction of policewomen, in her case, in both the USA and Britain (Schulz, 1995a). What is striking about these pioneer days is that there were, even by the 1920s, only very few women in policing anywhere in the world, yet they were far outnumbered by their supporters who campaigned for them.

In the next phase, sometimes called the 'latency period' (Heidensohn 1992, p. 41), when women were established as officers in various agencies around the world, they came under various kinds of threat, to which the policewomen's movement continued to respond. In Britain, full powers were not granted to female officers until 1931 (Carrier 1988) after long and vigorous struggles and various inquiries and commissions. In the USA, Schulz (1995a) has documented the ways in which the pioneer policewomen attached themselves to social work organizations (and not those for law enforcement) and gained support from the growing women's clubs. In Australia, Prenzler (1997) shows that only a prolonged and determined drive by women's organizations plus the intervention of the State's first woman MP finally brought women into policing in Queensland.

Outside the English-speaking world, perhaps the most fascinating example of these trends is in Germany. There, the first women were appointed as police sisters in Cologne in 1902. By 1911, a Committee of Dutch women were able to commission a survey of women's work in policing across the German speaking world. For this study, Beaujon (1911) collected data on cities in Austria, Germany, Holland and Switzerland and compared and analyzed their tasks. However, by the 1920s, war and its aftermath had damaged this system and women from the British Women's Police Service were brought in, through the intervention of an Englishwoman concerned at the appalling conditions she had observed there. This experiment lasted only two years but in some ways typifies the policewomen's movement during this second phase of its history.

Policewomen were still employed in various agencies in the limited roles they had, in effect, helped, with their supporters, to create. Broadly, and with local variants, they carried out social work and social protection tasks. Children and women, as offenders or victims, were their clients; whatever the specifies of their assignments, they were distinguished from their male colleagues. In what we call the 'cops' countries, they were usually called 'officers'; in Britain they wore uniforms, in some parts of Australia they had equal pay. Almost everywhere, recruits were drawn from among educated, professional women, at a time when their male counterparts came from the working class (and were recent migrants such as the Irish in the USA) and had minimal educational attainments (for many years the source of stereotyped jokes in Britain).

In Europe, which we characterized as having gendarmeries, women were mostly 'police sisters' or matrons at this period, as in Sweden. In defeated, occupied Germany after World War I when a

British model was introduced, the women officers too wore uniforms in some of the Länder. At this period, some of the colonial forces had no women officers, in Africa, for example. There was to be a repetition of the model adopted earlier in the setting up of a women's police in Germany after the First World War. Senior women officers from the Metropolitan Police were despatched to newly independent nations such as Tanzania to establish recruitment and training of women officers. As such, this phase can be characterized by continued international missionary activity. At this stage, while support for policewomen continued to flourish *outside* police agencies, some women had gained enough actual experience to promote the cause from that perspective. Alice Stebbins Wells, America's first policewoman, undertook lecture tours on this basis; *The Policewoman's Review*, a journal published in London during the 1920s and 1930s, records numerous journeys undertaken by Mary Allen, one of the British pioneers, to Europe (including Finland, Germany, Hungary and Poland). In addition, there were formally established international committees linked to the League of Nations and other bodies which brought together supporters of policewomen who believed they would help solve problems of vice, trafficking and related issues.

The rise of fascism and the outbreak of war once again impacted dramatically on the future of women in policing. For women in 'cop' countries, it was on the whole a stimulus to their role as social upheaval once more required their intervention. However, by this time, while there was still external enthusiasm, there were important shifts occurring.

In the USA, Schulz argues (1995a), policing only really became full time and professionalized in the twentieth century. Once that had happened, older style 'social worker' female officers could not survive. At the same time, in any case, feminist 'amateurs' were fading as the Depression hit them and policewomen had to look to new organizations for assistance.

Numbers of women recruited into law enforcement began to rise around the world *before* second-wave feminism, with its effects on formal legislation for equality, had begun to take hold. Some of the gendarmeries which had only had either police sisters or matrons established a more modern role for policewomen in the 1950s (Sweden and the Netherlands). West Germany was once again the site for missions for Britain, with British policewomen (on this occasion, seconded serving officers) setting up a service there.

English-speaking countries expanded recruitment and, informally, the role of women officers (Heidensohn 1992). As at so many phases of this story, outside factors, such as low pay (which dampened male recruitment figures in Britain), played their part.

This period ended with the shift in the main 'cops' countries to integration and formal equality in policing. Formal equality legislation in the USA and Britain was a key factor, as were wider issues, such as the political impact of the new women's movement (Heidensohn 1992). We have outlined how law enforcement agencies move through a series of stages to reach 'integration' which is, so far, the endstate. To do so, their time frames were sometimes telescoped and sometimes they have, as in some transitional and colonial nations, experienced double running, where women can be expected to carry out both a traditional segregated *and* an integrated role at the same time. The impact of integration has been widely discussed, although its introduction was not always carefully planned; it is, nevertheless, often forgotten that the distinctive tasks carried out by pre-integration women officers were frequently simply cast aside. Only much later, as issues such as domestic violence, physical and sexual abuse of children and of women, became matters of increasing public concern, were they addressed again seriously. This marked a most significant and perhaps poignant point for the original pioneers of policing for women: they had, in effect, invented a new form of social control. They had situated inside traditional law enforcement agencies a kind of cuckoo, an alien form which required the same form and framework as the parent body, yet which acted in a different way and came from distinct stock. This was all discarded with little foresight; some aspects of it have subsequently had to be reinvented or rediscovered. The external support which had for so long encouraged and upheld the role of women officers had already mostly disappeared. From this period on, the global links for policewomen, as well as local encouragement, has had to come from *within* the police. In most countries which we have studied, an integrated role is the one which forces choose for their twenty-first century policewomen. When they come relatively late to recruiting women, they generally address the question as though there can only be one outcome, that of full equality, as is the case in Austria, only taking on women in the 1980s (see *ENP Newsletter* 1997). We have found a few examples such as Brazil and India, where women-only police stations have been introduced, in order to make the reporting of crimes (such as rape) easier.

Achieving equality is another remarkable example of the convergence and synchronicity of much of the history of this field. Thus
parallel developments occurred in several agencies at about the
same time. Notably at this period, governments themselves pushed
this cause. In Sweden, Holland and Britain, the push came from an
outside agency, often with the police resisting firmly. At a later
stage, the 'cause' of promoting the role of policewomen was boosted
indirectly in several states by scandals associated with corruption
(the USA, Australia, Britain and Belgium) and brutality. A scenario
we have called elsewhere 'desperate remedies' can develop where
women are called upon to fill certain roles because confidence in
their male colleagues has fallen.

Policing and gender

We have already hinted that women came into law enforcement
originally to police their own sex. Taking both care and control of
the lives of others, especially in the 'private' areas of sexual and
domestic behaviour, were central themes of the pioneers of women's
role in policing. This fitted into a pattern of middle-class women
coming into a 'new' profession and transforming it. In the case of
policing, only the 'new' tasks represented novelty; there was a trans-
plant of these but it did not take well and the 'rejection' was massive.
Policewomen developed their work in this area for twice as long as
the period since integration. The history of policewomen can often be
divided up between the pre- and post-integration phases. During the
first era, the control of their own sex was seen as their primary task; it
was then discarded in many jurisdictions, where respondents to our
research often reported the problems they had in response.
    During the 1995 Beijing UN Conference on the position of
women, the issue of domestic violence occurred as a key topic,
and the European Network of Policewomen supported it as one of
their key projects (ENP 1995). Some of our respondents wished to
escape from these concerns, but others agreed to the adoption of
key targets which closely resembled some of those of the pre-integration phase. Tension still recurs for the police around these questions. A further and related issue, much voiced during our study,
was that of the abuse of female officers – their victimization, in
effect, by colleagues who harass them and *in extremis* drive them
from the force.

In the same way that not all women are domestically abused, not all policewomen suffer sexual harassment. What is argued is that the organizational structures, gender ratio and male-constructed images of police and policing create an environment that has parallels to domestic relationships in which men maintain control by being patronizing, violent or paternalistic. The reasons for policemen's reluctance to be drawn into policing violent behaviour perpetrated on women by men lie in attitudes that somehow women deserve it, ask for it or enjoy it. A policewoman as the victim may be 'deserving' in some manner by, for example, the nature or seriousness of her injuries, in which case police officers are sympathetic. But if the victim is undeserving, for example, a potential competitor for a promotion or specialist posting, and thus a possible troublemaker, then she must be put in her place and the power differential preserved. The persistence of these attitudes provides a measure of explanation about instances of sexual harassment that occur within the police. The structural realities of a male majority in control of resources within the police mirror those in domestic relationships. Women's investment in either job or home can make it difficult to leave; rather, some adaptation takes place. The cost of adapting to the police occupational culture for women can be adoption of a style that minimizes her professionalism or her femininity.

Comparative research

One of our main concerns in this book has been with the context of comparative research on policing around the world. We have developed and modified accepted models used by other scholars for this purpose and believe that this schema is worth examining in its own right and has value for application in further studies. We also maintain that our research speaks to key themes in the analysis of police culture. For example, Waddington has argued that this is a rhetorical matter, essentially harmless. Our study confirms the findings of others that, on the contrary, female officers can be intimidated by their colleagues and their health and career can be undermined.

Our methodologies also have something to say about research in this area, and indeed other areas of inquiry: thus we think they are worthy of further exploration. The example of the 'tip over' percentage share of women in positions in an organization is one where we believe we have made a contribution to an ongoing debate. The gender neutrality of Kanter's topological model of minority/majority ratios in workplaces has already been challenged. We found that there is no bureaucratizing out of discrimination and harassment by dint of numbers alone. The dynamics are more complicated than suggested by a strict application of Kanter's formula. We also retested the conceptualizations developed by one of us (FH) and tied these into a more complex model incorporating structural dimensions as well as cross-cultural comparison. The utility of this model, we believe, has been demonstrated and applied effectively in the present study.

Key issues in policing

The millennium era could justly be described as one of 'twentieth century blues': concern about policing has been nearly universal. At national and system levels, huge changes have been attempted, for example, in Eastern Europe and South Africa, to alter the whole agencies. Key problems have surfaced in numerous reports on corruption and other central issues (Newburn 1999) (Saulsbury *et al.* eds, 1996). Quite often, such studies ignore or marginalize gender. In summarizing aspects of our argument, we suggest that, in fact, our material has much to offer those considering these central themes.

Changing police culture has been of great concern (Chan 1997; Macpherson 1999) since so many law enforcement agencies have been troubled by it. Our data suggests that there can be some impact on the traditional culture but this is limited. We reflect too on the paradox of the most liberal regimes reporting the most harassment.

Two related sub-themes threading through much of the literature are: accountability and corruption. Our interviewees have much to say about these and how they might be dealt with. Many of them point to the breaking of basic rules, for example, on fair treatment and report what are, in effect, crimes committed within their agency. They also outline conditions for success. Some had experienced racism in their careers and discussed its structural and other sources, as well as sophisticated management responses.

Types of police organization

We noted that the various attempts to classify law enforcement practices mostly ignored women. Several modern authors who have tried to develop taxonomies of police systems have followed Fosdick's early lead and recognized the English/Continental divide. Bayley's threefold typology described 'authoritarian, oriental and Anglo Saxon' forms of policing. The first of these parallels the continental form and is essentially a military model, while the second, based on Bayley's own research on Japan, emphasizes close community ties. Mawby adapted Bayley's framework and developed a classification that included exported, colonial models. Explorations of colonial policing, tended to focus on former British colonies in 'New Commonwealth' countries. Britain introduced, not the 'policing by consent' approach of the home country, but, the centralized, more militaristic system which had its prototype in the Royal Irish Constabulary. Australia, New Zealand and, to some extent, Canada, were 'settler' states since immigration was a significant source of population growth which eventually dominated the indigenous peoples. In these nations, the parallels and shared culture with British policing are notable. Indeed, this has continued with British expertize being used to develop post colonial policing in Africa and, most recently, in the newly democratized states from the former Eastern Bloc. Peter Ryan, a senior British police officer, was appointed as the Commissioner for New South Wales in 1996 to reform that force.

We suggest that it is both helpful and instructive to look at the experiences of women in law enforcement around the world through comparative frames. The first of these we called 'cops', a model of policing by consent. For the second model, we adopted the 'gendarmes' applied to European continental and authoritarian systems which have military forms or origins. We retained a category we called 'colonial', borne as military models but adapted and modernized by a hybridization of ideas from the US and Britain. We added a further form 'transitional', those police forces emerging from totalitarian governments in Eastern Europe.

Policing models and policing women

When we examine specific areas of discrimination and harassment of women police, we can demonstrate differential rates of reporting.

Women cops appear to experience greatest discrimination in terms of deployment opportunities and, more than in other types of policing, face limitations on training opportunities and also are the most likely to report experiencing sexual harassment. However, women from the transitional forces are the most likely to report facing promotion blockage and restricted overtime opportunities. Generally speaking, women serving in Western continental forces, the gendarmes are the least likely to report discriminatory experiences. Women serving in forces having a colonial history are less likely to report discrimination than the cops or transitionals but more likely than the gendarmes.

We can then offer some speculative suggestions that attitudes and behaviours towards police women are reflected in the style of policing offered to women generally. Mawby (1999c p. 189) states that the British and American response both started with feminist critiques of the police's handling of rape and domestic violence, but then diverged in terms of solutions. In the UK, interventions by rape crisis centres and refuges were essentially in opposition to the police whereas in the USA, these groups co-operated with law-enforcement agencies. However, in Britain more recently, policing policies have moved together with interagency co-operation which includes the voluntary sector. The other development has been a pro-arrest policy whereby the police have powers to arrest the perpetrator of the violence without the active co-operation of the victim. This can be a rather punitive approach.

If we examine the delivery of services to victimized women within these different policing organizations, we can suggest from the preliminary indications from our data that cops and colonial types of forces, who have relatively high levels of reported sexual harassment within forces, are at a stage of awareness, often as a result of *cause célèbre* and successful lobbying campaigns. There is a recognition of the problem of sexualized violence and there are attempts to develop procedures and policies. The Metropolitan Police pioneered a scheme of sexual offences investigations officers (SOIT) and a chaperone scheme but evaluations revealed that chaperones were infrequently used and the workload fell disproportionately onto a few officers. The chaperones themselves perceived that their work was given low importance. Nixon (1992) reported that police officers in New South Wales may dismiss complaints of rape through stereotypic thinking and described the introduction of initial response officers to raise awareness and challenge attitudes. Perhaps the most telling indictment of police attitudes was Nixon's assertion that many police officers would not encourage their daughters to pursue a complaint of rape through the criminal justice system. Transitionals' police organizations, which have relatively high levels of discrimination, appear to have fairly primitive notions still about the policing of domestic violence. A Russian policewoman from our study writes: 'With the exception of very serious forms of abuse like homicides violence against women remained unnoticed. It was not possible to criticize the treatment of raped or abused women by the police or doctors through the official channels.' In Hungary, 'domestic violence against women is neither the focus of attention of criminal justice, nor in the limelight of social interest' (Sarkozi 1994). Bowdler (1998) notes that in Poland, battered wives are beginning to speak out about domestic violence and the first national help line has been established. The organizer of the help line indicated that Poland is twenty years behind the West in dealing with these issues.

In the gendarmes, which have relatively lower levels of reported discrimination and lower rates of sexual harassment, policy development and practice is variable with something of a North South divide: Northern European police forces generally being more developed than their Southern European counterparts.

Table 7.1 Policing models, reported impact on police women and women's victimization

Type of police organization	Sex discrimination	Sexual harassment	Women's victimization
Cops	high	high	High levels of awareness, policy developed, variable interventions: inter agency, service based and/or punitive
Colonial history	low	high	Moderate awareness, policy developed, ambivalent implementation
Transitionals	high	low	Low levels of awareness, little policy development and negative practice
Gendarmes	low	low	Variable policy development and practice

Wider issues

Some of our findings – for instance, those on gender in organizations – are significant for fields other than police research. We have already noted the critique of Kanter's work and the impact of gender ratio on discrimination. Worth drawing attention to as well is the importance of various coping strategies used by the policewomen in their work and the potency of the occupational culture. We have also attempted some innovative research techniques (in areas where it is difficult to gain access to materials or respondents) that could be adopted in other difficult research areas.

Research, including studies of gender, is increasingly global in character. Our study has tried to offer the first truly international analytical perspective on the issue of gender in policing. Paradoxically, this was a topic which first gained status as an international phenomenon, consciously promoted by determined pioneers. Their heirs face a different twenty-first century world, but one where, perhaps for the first time, some of that curious vision might be realized.

Appendix 1: Discourse Analysis used in Chapter 3[*]

It is not intended here to give a detailed account of the method of Discourse Analysis, as a brief technical appendix would not do justice to the complexities of the approach. A helpful grounding in the theoretical basis and practical application is available in Wetherell and Potter (1992) and a neat worked example providing an analysis of the absence of women DJs on radio is provided by Gill (1993). Rather, some additional explanation is offered to supplement the discussion in Chapter 3.

Much of the source material used by Discourse Analysts is text, either written accounts or transcripts of interviews. The focus is language and use of linguistic devices such as justification, accusation, blaming, questioning, which are conceived as social practices in themselves. Of the myriad ways to express thoughts and descriptions, what is of particular interest is the manner of expression and the meanings it is intended to convey. In our case, we make use of historical texts and illustrative materials, namely cartoons. As cartoons often exaggerate and accentuate traits, physical characteristics and situations, it can be argued that it is easier to 'read' the underlying social reality, that is, the belief that women are inherently unsuited to the task of policing.

Edwards and Potter (1992, p.28) note in their approach to Discourse Analysis that text should be naturally occurring. We obtained extracts of written texts from official reports, such as annual reports of Her Majesty's Inspectorates of Constabulary; police magazines such as *The Police Review*, *The Policewoman's Review*, Police Union/Staff Associations' monthly periodicals. Our source materials included minutes, letters, photographs and cartoons. We cannot claim that our searches were exhaustive or that we sampled a representative selection of materials in order to conduct our analyses. We did examine the annual volumes of publications, in the case of *Police Review* spanning some one hundred years. In general, there was a dearth of references to policewomen and the examples we found were the result of careful scanning of the annual index when this was available. Where not, we laboriously went through each issue to locate appropriate cartoons or letters. We were also sent cartoons by colleagues who knew of our interest.

---

[*] We are grateful to Rebecca Horn for her commentary on Chapter 3 and have used some of her observations in this appendix.

Once we had a collection of materials, these were organized chronologic-
ally and a 'reading' of both text and cartoons was undertaken. We had no *a
priori* classification system; rather, we looked for emergent themes. We
looked particularly at the physical representation of policewomen and
looked for the constructive devices used to account for policewomen's
performance (or non performance) of police duties. We discovered much
of the purposes of our texts was to deprofessionalize or defeminize policewomen in order to justify their exclusion from policing. This was accomplished by use of claims such as those of nature which dictate demarcated
roles for men and women.

As Discourse Analysis is concerned with the latent as well as manifest
content, we were particularly interested in the use of names such as Eve,
decoy Doras, Doris, Doreen and Shirley which have various metaphorical
connotations.

Ours was very much a voyage of discovery. We wanted to situate
attitudes and behaviour towards policewomen historically in order to
attempt some understanding of the contemporary resistance to women
officers. We were trying in Chapter 3 to address the construction of a
rhetoric about policewomen. Here it is the construction of the rhetoric
that was of interest, not the accuracy of the portrayal. Chapter 4 attempts
some evaluation of the actual performance and impact of women on
policing.

The Discourse Analysis seemed particularly helpful in drawing out the
conflicts and contradictions of the constructed image of women police
officers. What was of especial interest was the apparent simultaneous
holding of conflicting beliefs. Thus, images are presented of policewoman
as purifier, saviour, temptress, matron, radical, helper, fighter, macho,
dyke. The paradox of these simultaneous representations is that it is
impossible for policewomen to succeed because their strengths are neutral-
ized by an opposition. She is purifier and temptress, reformer and con-
server. A further paradox evident in the rhetoric is that policewomen are
somehow different to other women but that all women are actually the
same. Policemen need to be protected by policewomen, for example, when
interviewing female victims, but also need to be protected from policewomen who are dangerous seductresses. We can peel another layer from
this when examining the role of women as agent provocateurs harnessed in
the service of undercover investigations: a further example of the no-win
situation where women are condemned for the very qualities that are
useful.

The cartoons particularly reiterate the theme of threat posed by women
to the hegemonic construction of masculinity. For policemen to maintain
their control over policing, they need to see women as something very
different and to preserve policing as a male occupation. If women police
efficiently and effectively, both beliefs are challenged. The undercurrent of

several cartoons is either emasculation or castration which is an explicit reference to fears of emasculation which must be fought off at all costs. The power of the cartoons not only lies with those doing the constructing (and show remarkable persistence over time) but are projected into the work environment which makes policewomen's actual behaviour relatively ineffectual at changing attitudes.

References

Gill, R. (1993) 'Justifying injustice: broadcasters' accounts of inequality in radio', in Burman, E. and Parker, I. (eds.) *Discourse analytic research; repertoires and readings of texts in action* (London: Routledge).

Edwards, D. and Potter, J. (1992) *Discursive psychology* (London: Sage).

Wetherell, M. and Potter, J. (1993) *Mapping the language of racism: discourse and the legitimation of exploitation* (New York: Harvester Wheatsheaf).

Appendix 2: Questionnaire Survey

BIRMINGHAM CONFERENCE '96

We would be most grateful if you could spare some time to fill in this questionnaire. Hopefully, some results will be made available at the Conference.

Professor Frances Heidensohn
Goldsmiths College
London University, SE14 6NW, UK

Dr Jennifer Brown
Hampshire Constabulary
Winchester, SO22 5DB, UK

1. In which country do you serve as a law enforcement officer?

2. How long have you served as a law enforcement officer? ☐☐ years

3. How old are you ☐☐ years

4. Are you

    male ☐

    female ☐

5. Are you

    single ☐

    married/living as married ☐

    divorced ☐

    widowed ☐

6. Are you

    White/caucasian ☐

    Black ☐

    Hispanic ☐

    Asian ☐

    other ☐

7. Do you have children?

    no ☐

    children living at home ☐

    children not at home ☐

8. Do you have a university degree?

    Yes ☐

    No ☐

9. Is your work mostly

    patrol ☐

    investigation ☐

    training ☐

    administration ☐

    traffic ☐

    operational support ☐

    other ☐

10. What is your rank/grade?

11. How many men and women officers are there in your work unit?

    men ☐☐

    women ☐☐

12. Do you think you are fully accepted as an equal

a) by all your male officers   ☐   b) by all female officers   ☐

     most male officers   ☐   most female officers   ☐

     some male officers   ☐   some female officers   ☐

     few male officers   ☐   few female officers   ☐

     none   ☐   none   ☐

13. Have you experienced discrimination in the following areas

                                        Yes   No

     a) promotion   ☐   ☐

     b) deployment/work assignments   ☐   ☐

     c) training   ☐   ☐

     d) overtime payments   ☐   ☐

14. Have you experienced any sexual harassment from officer colleagues at work from *either*

a) male officer colleagues   and / or   b) female officer colleagues

     never   ☐   never   ☐

     rarely   ☐   rarely   ☐

     sometimes   ☐   sometimes   ☐

     often   ☐   often   ☐

15. How have you personally coped with discrimination/harassment. *Please tick as many as appropriate*

     a) saying nothing   ☐

     b) joking   ☐

     c) being assertive   ☐

     d) being aggressive   ☐

     e) complaining to a more senior officer   ☐

     f) seeking help from your union/staff association   ☐

     g) some other   ☐   ☐

16. Does your organisation have equal opportunities policy/procedure

                                        Yes   ☐

                                        No   ☐

17. Please indicate if your career has been advanced through help by any of the following

		Yes	No
a)	a supportive female officer colleague	☐	☐
b)	a supportive female senior officer	☐	☐
c)	a supportive male officer colleague	☐	☐
d)	a supportive male senior officer	☐	☐
e)	proving yourself by working harder than colleagues	☐	☐
f)	developing some additional skills/qualification	☐	☐
g)	equal opportunities policies/practice in your organisation	☐	☐
h)	your union/staff association	☐	☐

18. Please can you circle the appropriate number to indicate how highly you agree or disagree with each of the following

		Agree strongly	Agree	Neither agree nor disagree	Disagree	Disagree strongly
a)	If I can't do a job the first time I keep trying until I can	1	2	3	4	5
b)	I avoid trying to learn new things when they look too difficult for me	1	2	3	4	5
c)	I give up easily	1	2	3	4	5
d)	I seem capable of dealing with most problems that come up in life	1	2	3	4	5
e)	I find I make new friends easily	1	2	3	4	5
f)	I do not know how to handle new situations	1	2	3	4	5

19. Do you work in a

police department	☐
marshal's office	☐
corrections	☐
BATF	☐
other, please specify	☐ _____

20. Would you mind being contacted again

		Yes	No
a)	to be interviewed whilst at the conference	☐	☐
b)	receive a longer questionnaire to complete	☐	☐

21. If so please give us your name and address

Name: _____

Contact address: _____

_____

_____

Telephone number: _____

Thank you very much for your help. Results of this questionnaire will be reported as general trends. No individual will be identified.

If you have any other comments you would like to make please add them below.

Please return the questionnarie with your conference registration papers, or to a representative of the British Association of Women Police.

Appendix 3: Countries Served in by the Survey Sample Reported in Chapter 5

Country	N (per cent)
Australia	206 (26%)
USA	186 (23%)
England and Wales	76 (9%)
Northern Ireland	62 (8%)
Canada	43 (5%)
Republic of Ireland	38 (5%)
Luxembourg	29 (4%)
Malawi	26 (3%)
Netherlands	19 (2%)
Belgium	17 (2%)
Germany	16 (2%)
Botswana	12 (1.5%)
Finland	11 (1%)
Poland	11 (1%)
Sweden	9 (1%)
New Zealand	7 (1%)
France	5 (1%)
Switzerland	4 (1%)
Cyprus	4 (1%)
Denmark	3 (1%)
Hungary	3 (1%)
Romania	2 (1%)
Kazakhstan	2 (1%)
Moldova	2 (1%)
Estonia	2 (1%)
Norway	1 (1%)
Spain	1 (1%)
Lithuania	1 (1%)
Russia	1 (1%)
Ukraine	1 (1%)
Iceland	1 (1%)
Israel	1 (1%)
Malta	1 (1%)
Missing data	1 (1%)
Total	804

Appendix 4: Statistical Details of Time-based Comparison Reported in Chapter 5

Measures	Elders	Seasoned	Fledgling	ANOVA F	Chi Square	p value
Gender ratio	20.08	16.59	18.49	1.85		0.16ns
Self-efficacy	18.40	18.43	18.13	1.02		0.36ns
Mean male acceptance	2.20	2.06	2.16	1.55		0.21ns
Mean female acceptance	1.57	1.49	1.56	0.70		0.50ns
Mean discrimination	1.39	0.98	0.83	11.0		0.00***
% discrimination						
promotion	31.5%	20.9%	19.7%		8.39	0.02*
deployment	57.9%	49.2%	33.3%		17.54	0.00***
training	36.8%	24.8%	23.2%		10.01	0.00***
overtime	18.1%	12.8%	19.9%		2.29	0.32ns
Mean male harassment	2.39	2.11	1.60		28.22	0.00***
Mean female harassment	1.26	1.10	1.10		6.48	0.00***
% Coping mechanisms						
say nothing	54.6%	30.3%	26.3%			0.00***
joking	59.0%	52.5%	19.7%			0.00***
assertive	64.2%	47.5%	10.5%			0.00***
aggressive	23.6%	13.1%	11.8%			0.00***
complain	27.8%	13.1%	26.3%			0.00***
union	12.2%	4.9%	17.1%			0.02*
other	17.4%	4.9%	9.2%			0.00***
Mean coping	2.47	2.09	1.86	40.75		0.00***
% Support strategies						
female colleague	43.2%	31.5%	26.7%		8.68	0.01**
female senior	34.9%	23.9%	22.8%		6.10	0.05*
male colleague	59.9%	61.5%	36.1%		13.25	0.00***
male senior	67.3%	51.2%	33.9%		31.62	0.00***

Measures	Elders	Seasoned	Fledgling	ANOVA F	Chi Square	p value
work harder	80.7%	68.7%	51.4%		33.42	0.00***
extra skills	82.4%	73.8%	50.0%		37.93	0.00***
EO practice	41.9%	42.0%	41.1%		0.02	0.99ns
Union	17.6%	14.3%	9.3%		2.70	0.26ns
Mean support	3.36	2.09	1.86	44.37		0.00***

Note: ns not statistically significant * p < .05 ** p < .01 *** p < .001

Appendix 5: Qualitative Interviews Forming the Basis of Analysis Reported in Chapter 6

In an effort to triangulate the results of the survey and to amplify our understanding of the quantitative results, we undertook a series of more detailed qualitative interviews at one of the conference sites, Birmingham 1996. As Heidensohn (1997) previously observed:

> We realized at an early stage that we should have to plan carefully in order to achieve at least our aim of a minimum of over twenty interviews. At the same time we recognized that our approach had to be highly flexible to take advantage of interview opportunities as they arose. It was clear that we should need assistance and we were fortunately able to recruit three additional interviewers...All had relevant previous experience and had interviewed police officers. We held a series of planning meetings during the earlier months of 1996 and devised a strategy to take maximum advantage of the opportunity offered by the conference. This included: producing publicity material (to be mailed to delegates) identifying us all as the research road show; liaising with the conference organizers to ensure facilities; setting up an introduction party for the first evening to which we invited potential interviewees.

> We also developed interview checklists, cover sheets and a series of targets for interviewees from different countries and regions. For instance, we were especially keen to contact and interview officers from areas which are normally hard to reach and/or those on which little or no research material has been published...In the weeks before the conference we held training and briefing sessions in London where we rehearsed the interview schedule, discussed practical details.

> During the actual conference we endeavored to maintain a diary so that interview engagements could be kept. While we kept to our dates as far as we could, some officers failed to appear or were elusive. One or two took time to agree to respond and with one national group, the team felt that they were wary of their (male) senior officer and were unwilling to participate.

In the light of some of our respondents' concerns about being identified, we have given only sketchy details of where they served and limited demographic details in order to preserve their anonymity.

The present analysis is based on 47 respondents from 19 countries. Direct quotations are given from interviews with officers from a range of countries as listed in the table below.

Demographic and occupational details of the interview sample

Average Age	39.8 years
Average length of service	18.6 years
Rank	
Constable	13%
Supervisor	77%
Duties	
Uniform patrol	40%
Detective	21%
HQ	11%
Traffic	6%
Child protection	6%
Personnel	6%
Training	4%
Immigration	2%
Interpol liaison	2%
Respondent number as appears in Chapter 6	**Country in which respondent(s) serve as a police officer**
1, 2, 3, 4	England and Wales
7, 8	Scotland
10, 11, 13, 15, 16, 17, 21	USA
22, 23	Canada
26	Uganda
27	Philippines
30	Malawi
31	Botswana
33	Trinidad
34, 35, 36	Sweden
37, 38, 39	Netherlands
40	Iceland
42	Switzerland
43	Germany
44	Russia
47	Poland
48	Papua New Guinea
49	New Zealand

Thus our interview sample was slightly older (40 years compared with 35 years) and had served marginally longer than our survey sample (19 years compared with 12 years). The interview respondents were also more senior than the survey sample (77% were supervisory officers compared with 48%).

Reference

Heidensohn, F. (1997) 'Sisters and strangers'. Paper presented to the American Society of Criminology Meeting, San Diego, California, November.

References

Adler, Z. (1990a) 'Hill street clues; the US police record on promoting women', *Personnel Management*. August, pp. 28–33.

Adler, Z. (1990b) *A fairer cop: the US police record on equal opportunities* (London: Wainright Trust).

Ahire, P. (1991) *Imperial policing* (Milton Keynes: Open University Press).

Aleem, S. (1989) 'Women in policing in India', *Police Studies*, **12**, pp. 97–103.

Alimo-Metcalfe, B. (1993) 'A woman's ceiling; a man's floor', *Health Service Journal* 14 October, pp. 25–7.

Allen, K. (1997) 'A study of the career progression of male and female police officers in Bedfordshire'. Dissertation submitted to Birkbeck College, University of London.

Allen, M. (1925) *The pioneer policewoman* (London: Chatto and Windus).

Anderson, D. M. and Killingray, D. (eds.) (1991) *Policing the empire; government, authority and control* 1983–1940 (Manchester: Manchester University Press).

Anderson, D. M. and Killingray, D. (eds.) (1992) *Policing and decolonialization; politics, nationalism and the police* 1917–1965 (Manchester: Manchester University Press).

Anderson, M., den Boer, M., Cullen, P., Gilmore, W., Raab, C. and Walker, N. (1995) *Policing the European Union* (Oxford: Clarendon Press).

Anderson, R., Brown, J. and Campbell, E. A. (1993) *Aspects of sex discrimination in police forces in England and Wales* (London: Home Office Police Research Group).

Austin, W. (1996) 'The Socialization of women police: male officer hostility to female officers'. Paper given at First Australasian Women Police Conference Sydney, 29–31 July.

Balkin, J. (1988) 'Why policemen don't like police women', *Journal of Police Science and Administration* **16**, pp. 29–38.

Bandura, A. (ed.) (1995) *Self efficacy in changing societies* (Cambridge: Cambridge University Press).

Bayley, D. H. (1982) 'A world perspective on the role of the police in social control', in Donelan, R. (ed.) *The maintenance of order in society* (Ottawa: Canadian Police College)

Bayley, D. H. (1985) *The future of policing* (Oxford: Oxford University Press).

Bayley, D. H. (1994) *Police for the future* (New York: Oxford University Press).

Bayley, D. H. (1999) 'Policing: the World Stage', in Mawby, R. (ed.).
Baxter, R. (1943) *Women of the Gestapo* (London: Morrison and Gibb).
Beaujon, C. W. (1911) *Die Mitarbeit der Frau bei der Polizei* (Utrecht: Kluiver).
Becke, S. (1973) 'Metropolitan Police uni-sex', *Police Journal*, XIVI, pp. 274–9.
Becker, S, and Stephens, M. (eds.) (1994) *Police force police service* (London: Macmillan).
Beckman, E. (1980) *Law enforcement in a democratic society* (New York: Nelson Hall).
Bell, D. Z. (1982) 'Policewomen; myth and reality', *Journal of Police Science and Administration*, 10, pp. 112–20.
Belmans, J. (1994) 'Women against organised crime'. Paper presented to the 3rd International Conference of the European Network for Police-women. Belgium, 21–24 November.
Benyon, J., Turnbull, L., Willis, A., Woodward, R. and Beck, A. (1993) *Police co-operation in Europe: an investigation* (University of Leicester: Centre for the Study of Public Order).
Benyon, J. *et al.* (1995) *Police forces in the new European Union: a conspectus* (University of Leicester: Centre for the Study of Public Order).
Berg, B. L. and Budnick, K. J. (1986) 'Defeminization of women in law enforcement', *Journal of Police Science and Administration*, 14, pp. 314–19.
Bittner, E. (1990) *Aspects of police work* (Boston, MA: North Eastern University Press).
Boni, N. (1998) *Deployment of women in policing* (Paymeham S.A.: National Police Research Unit).
Borg, I. (ed.) (1981) *Multidimensional data representation, when and why* (Ann Arbor MI: Mathesis).
Bowdler, N. (1998) 'Polish women awake from silent suffering', *The Guardian* February 7 p. 14.
Bratton, W. J. (1997) 'Crime is down in New York: blame the police', in Dennis, N. (ed) *Zero tolerance: policing a free society* (London: IEA Health and Welfare Unit).
Bratton, W. J., Dennis, N. and Griffiths, W. (1997) *Zero tolerance: policing a free society* (London: LEA).
Breakwell, G. (1979) 'Woman: group and identity?', *Women's Studies International Quarterly*, 2, pp. 9–17.
Breakwell, G. (1986) *Coping with threatened identities* (London: Methuen).
Breakwell. G. (1992) 'Processes and self evaluation; efficacy and estrange-ment', in Breakwell, G. (ed.) *Social psychology of identity and the self concept* (London: Surrey University Press in association with Harcourt Brace Jovanovich).
Brewer, J. (1991a) *Inside the RUC: policing in a divided community* (Oxford: Clarendon).

Brewer, J. (1991b) 'Hercules, Hippolyte and the Amazons', *British Journal of Sociology*, **42**, pp. 231–47.

Brewer, J., Guelke, A., Hume, I., Moxon-Browne, E. and Wilford, R. (1996) *The police, public order and the state* (Basingstoke: Macmillan).

Brogden, M. (1987) 'The emergence of the police: the colonial dimension', *British Journal of Criminology*, **27**(1), pp. 4–15.

Brooks, L., and Perot, A. A. (1991) 'Reporting sexual harassment; exploring a predictive model', *Psychology of Women Quarterly*, **15**, pp. 31–47.

Brown, M. (1994) 'The plight of female police: a survey of NW patrolmen', *Police Chief*, **91**, pp. 50–53.

Brown, J. (1994) 'Equality environment in the Central Scotland Police'. Paper presented to an equal opportunities seminar, Stirling: Central Scotland Police, 12–13 May.

Brown, J. (1995) 'Networking in Europe', *Newsletter of the European Network*, **1**, pp. 2–4.

Brown, J. (1996) 'Abusive relationships at work: explaining the police's response to sexual harassment by an analysis of their attitudes to rape and domestic violence', in *gender and life in organizations*, Occasional Paper 5, Department of Business and Management. University of Portsmouth.

Brown, J. (1997) 'Women in policing: a comparative research perspective', *International Journal of the Sociology of Law*, **25**, pp. 1–19.

Brown, J. M. (1998) 'Aspects of discriminatory treatment of women police officers serving in forces in England and Wales', *British Journal of Criminology*, **38**, pp. 265–82.

Brown, J. and Campbell, E. A. (1991) 'Less than equal', *Policing*, **7**, pp. 324–33.

Brown, J., Campbell, E. A. and Fife Schaw, C. (1995) 'Adverse impacts experienced by police officers following exposure to sex discrimination and sexual harassment', *Stress Medicine*, **11**, pp. 221–8.

Brown, J. and Fielding J. (1993) 'Qualitative differences in men and women police officers' experience of occupational stress, *Work and Stress*, **7**, pp. 327–40.

Brown, J. M. and Gillick, M. (1998) 'Differing perspectives on a police force's equal opportunities grievance procedure', *International Journal of Police Science and Management*, **1**, pp. 122–32.

Brown, J. M. and Grover, J. (1997) 'Stress and the woman sergeant', *Police Journal*, **LXXI**, pp. 47–54.

Brown, J., Hazenberg, A. and Ormiston, C. (1999) 'Women in policing: an international comparison', in Mawby, R. (ed.) *Comparative policing* (London: UCL Press).

Brown, J. and Heidensohn, F. (1996) 'Exclusion orders', *Policing Today*, September 20–24.

Brown, J., Maidment, A. and Bull, R. (1992) 'Appropriate task matching or gender bias in deployment of male and female police officers?', *Policing & Society*, **2**, pp. 1–16.

Brown, J. and Neville, M. (1996) 'Arrest rate as a measure of police men and women's productivity and competence', *Police Journal*, **LXIX**(4), 299–307.

Brown, J. and Sargent, S. (1995) 'Policewomen and firearms', *Police Studies*, pp. 1–14.

Brown, J. M., and Waters, I. (1996) 'Force versus service', in Waddington, D. and Chritchner, C. (eds) *Public order policing* (Aldershot: Avebury).

Browne, A. (1995) 'Fear and the perception of alternatives; asking "why battered women don't leave" is the wrong question' in Raffel Price, B. and Sokoloff, N. (eds.) *The criminal justice system and women offenders victims and co-workers*, 2nd edn (New York: McGraw-Hill).

Bryant, L., Dunkerley, D. and Kelland, G. (1985) 'One of the boys?', *Policing*, **1**(4), pp. 236–44.

Burman, M. and Lloyd, S. (1993) *Specialist police units in the investigation of violent crime against women and children in Scotland* (Edinburgh: Scottish Office Central Research Unit).

Calderwood, A. (1974) *In service of the community* (Hong Kong: Liang Yo Printing).

Cameron, M. (1993) *Women in green* (Belfast: RUC Historical Society).

Campbell, B. (1993) *Goliath: Britain's dangerous places* (London: Methuen).

Carden, M. G. (n.d.) *Women patrols* (London: National Union of Women Workers of Great Britain).

Carrier, J. (1988) *The campaign for the employment of women as police officers* (Aldershot: Avebury/Gower).

Casey, E. (1992) 'Sexual harassment at work: the importance of the relationship between perpetrator and victim'. BSc Dissertation, University of Surrey.

Carter, I. (1993) 'Equality without grievance'. MA Dissertation, University of Hertfordshire.

Chan, J. (1996) 'Changing police culture', *British Journal of Criminology*, **36**, pp. 109–34.

Chan, J. (1997) *Changing police culture* (Cambridge: Cambridge University Press).

Chase, J. (1995) 'Historical analysis in psychological research', in Breakwell, G., Hammond, S. and Fife-Schaw, C. (eds) *Research methods in psychology* (London: Sage).

Cherrett, O. J. (1990) 'Without fear or favour: 150 years of policing Auckland 1840–1990', unpublished paper.

Cobut, E. (1994) 'The police services image with their internal and external customers'. Paper presented to the 3rd Annual Conference of the European Network of Policewomen, Brussels. 21–24 November.

Coffey, S., Brown, J. M. and Savage, P. (1992) 'Policewomen's career aspirations; some reflections on the roles and capabilities of British women officers', *Police Studies*, **15**, pp. 13–19.

Cole, B. (1999) 'Post colonial systems' in Mawby, R. (ed.) *Policing Across the world*.

Colson, E. (n.d.) 'Career development for women officers'. Bedfordshire Police unpublished report.

Corryn, S. (1994) 'Ongewenst seksueel gedrag op het werk geprojecteerd binnen de entiteit van gemeentelijk politie'. Gentbrugge: Police Academy of East Flanders.

Coyle, A. (1995) 'Discourse analysis', in Breakwell, G., Hammond, S. and Fife-Schaw, C. (eds.) *Research methods in psychology* (London: Sage).

Coyle, A. and Morgan-Sykes, C. (1998) 'Troubled men and threatened women; the construction of crisis in male mental health', *Feminism and Psychology*, **8**, pp. 263–84.

Daly, K. (1989) 'Criminal justice ideologies and practice in different voices; some feminist questions about justice', *International Journal of the Sociology of Law*, 17, pp. 1–18.

Daum, J. M. (1994) 'Police work from a woman's perspective', *Police Chief*, **91**(9), pp. 46–9.

Davies, S. (1994) 'Equality; to walk what we talk', *Policing Today*, **1**, pp. 26–9.

Dene, E. (1992) 'A comparison of the history of entry of women into policing to France and England and Wales', *Police Journal*, **65**, pp. 236–42.

Dennis, N. (ed.) (1997) *Zero tolerance: policing a free society* (London: IEA Health and Welfare Unit).

Eikenaar, L. (1993) 'Dat hoort er nu eenmaal bij... Aard en omvang van ongewenste omgangsvormen bij de Nederlandse Politie'. Amersfoort: Landelijke Politie Emancipatie Commissie.

Emsley, C. (1997) 'The history of crime and control institutions', in Maguire, M., Morgan, R. and Reiner, R. (eds) *The Oxford handbook of criminology* (Oxford: Oxford University Press).

Enhus, E. (1990) 'Kenmerken van politiewerk van politieorganisatie envan politiecultur'. School of Criminology VUB.

Equal Opportunities Commission (1990) *Managing to make progress* (London: Receiver for the Metropolitan Police).

European Network of Policewomen (1998) 'Policy Plan 1998–2000'. Amersfoort.

Everett, V. (1995) 'Equal opportunities survey summary'. Kent Constabulary unpublished report.

Felkenes, G. T. and Lasley, J. R. (1992) 'Implications of hiring women police officers: police administrators concepts may not be justified', *Policing and Society*, 3, pp. 41–50.

Fielding, N. (1988) *Joining forces: police training, socialization and occupational competence* (London: Routledge).

Fielding, N. (1994) 'Cop canteen culture', in Newburn, T. and Stanko, E. (eds) *Just boys doing business: men, masculinity and crime* (London: Routledge).

Fielding, N. G. and Fielding, J. L. (1987) 'A study of resignation during British Police training', *Journal of Police Science and Administration*, 15, pp. 24–36.

Fielding, N. and Fielding, J. (1992) 'A comparative minority: female recruits to a British constabulary force'. *Policing and Society*, 2, pp. 205–18.

Fijnaut, C. (1991) 'Police co-operation within Western Europe' in Heidensohn, F. M. and Farrell, M. (eds) *Crime in Europe* (London: Routledge).

Finnane, M. (1990) 'Police corruption and police reform: the Fitzgerald Inquiry in Queensland, Australia', *Policing and Society*, 1, pp. 59–71.

Fischer, M. and Gleijm, H. (1994) 'The gender gap in management; a challenging affair', *Newsletter of the European Network of Policewomen*, February, pp. 3–6.

Fiske, S. (1991) 'Expert testimony presented in Robinson *v*, US District Court Florida Division 482 US 301.

Fletcher, M. (1991) 'The integration of policewomen in the British police force: a national survey of male and female officers and former policewomen'. MSc Dissertation, University of Surrey.

Fosdick, R. (1915) *European Police Systems* Reprint 1969 (Montclair NJ: Patterson Smith).

French, M. and Waugh, L. (1998) 'The weaker sex? Women and police work. *International Journal of Police Science and Administration*', 1, pp. 260–75.

Frone, M. R., Russell, M. and Barnes, G. M. (1996) 'Work related conflict, gender and health related outcomes: a study of employed parents in two communities', *Journal of Occupational Health Psychology*, 1, pp. 37–69.

Giuliani, R. W. and Bratton, W. J. (1994) 'Police strategy no 5: reclaiming the public spaces of New York. New York: New York Police Department.

Glennerster, H. (1995) *British social policy since 1945* (Oxford: Blackwell).

Gooch, K. (1991) '(E)quality of service?' Cambridgeshire Constabulary unpublished report.

Gornall, M. (1972) 'The changing role of women in the police services of Britain and America', *Police College Magazine*, 13, pp. 38–44.

Gossett, J. L. and Williams, J. E. (1998) 'Perceived discrimination among women in law enforcement', *Women and Criminal Justice*, 10, pp. 53–73.

Graef, R. (1990) 'What's wrong with the police?', *Independent on Sunday*, 18 March.

Grant, N. K., Garrison, C. G. and McCormick, K. (1990) 'Perceived utilisation, job satisfaction and advancement of police women', *Public Personnel Management*, **19**(2), pp. 147–54.

Greater Manchester Police (1995) 'Sexual harassment survey'. Gender Issues Working Group. Unpublished report.

Gregory, J. (1987) *Sex, race and law* (London: Sage).

Grennan, S. (1987) 'Findings on the role of officer gender in violent encounters with citizens', *Journal of Police Science and Administration*, **15**, pp. 78–85.

Griffiths, W. (1997) Zero tolerance: a view from London, in Dennis, N. (ed) *Zero tolerance: policing a free society* (London: EA Health and Welfare Unit).

Gross, S. (1984) 'Women becoming cops: developmental issues and solutions', *Police Chief*, **51**, pp. 32–5.

Gütges, K. (1998) 'Policewomen before and after the fall of the "iron curtain" in Germany, a comparison', *ENP Newsletter*, **3**, pp. 2–4.

Halford, S., Savage, M. and Witz, A. (1997) *Gender, careers and organisations* (London: Macmillan).

Hammond, S. (1990) *Psychometric analysis package* (Guildford: University of Surrey).

Hatalak, O., Alvazzi Del Frate, A. and Zvekic, U. (1998) *The international crime victim survey in countries in transition* National Reports (Rome: UNICRI).

Hazenberg, A. and Kroeze, A. (eds) (1994) *Facts, figure and general information* (Amersfoort: European Network of Policewomen).

Hazenberg, A. and Ormiston, C. (1995) *Women in Europe: what's it all about?* (Amersfoort: European Network of Policewomen).

Hazenberg, A. and Ormiston, C. (1996) *World-wide policing: a woman's affair* (Amersfoort: European Network of Policewomen).

Hebenton, B. and Thomas, T. (1995) *Policing Europe – co-operation, conflict and control* (Basingstoke: Macmillan).

Heidensohn, F. (1968) 'The deviance of women: a critique and an enquiry', *British Journal of Sociology*, 19, pp. 160–75.

Heidensohn, F. (1986) 'Models of justice: Portia or Persephone? Some thoughts on equality, fairness and gender in the field of criminal justice', *International Journal of the Sociology of Law*, **14**, pp. 287–98.

Heidensohn, F. (1989) 'Women in policing in the USA'. Report to the Police Foundation.

Heidensohn, F. (1991) 'Introduction: convergence, diversity and change' in Heidensohn, F. M. and Farrell, M. (eds) *Crime in Europe* (London: Routledge).

Heidensohn, F. (1992) *Women in control? The role of women in law enforcement* (Oxford: Clarendon).

Heidensohn, F. (1994a) 'From being to knowing: some issues in the study of gender in contemporary society', *Women and Criminal Justice*, 6, pp. 13–37.

Heidensohn, F. (1994b) 'We can handle it out here: women officers in Britain and the USA and the policing of public order', *Policing and Society*, 4, pp. 293–303.

Heidensohn, F. (1996a) 'Making it even; equal opportunities and public order', in Critcher, C. and Waddington, D. (eds) *Policing public order: theoretical and practical issues* (Aldershot: Avebury).

Heidensohn, F. (1996b) 'The impact of police culture: setting the scene'. Paper presented to the First Australasian Women Police Conference, Sydney 29–31 July.

Heidensohn, F. (1996c) 'Comparing charges: comparative studies of policing and gender'. Paper presented to the Annual Meeting of the American Society of Criminology, 22 November.

Heidensohn, F. (1997) 'Crime and policing' in Symes, V. Levy, C. and Littlewood J. (eds) *The future of Europe* (London: Macmillan).

Heidensohn, F. M. (1998) 'Comparative models of policing and the role of women Officers'. *International Journal of Police Science and Management*, 1(3), pp. 215–26.

Heidensohn, F. M. (2000) *Sexual politics and social control* (Buckingham: Open University Press).

Heiskanen, M. and Piispa, M. (1998) *Faith, hope and battering*, Statistics. Helsinki.

Her Majesty's Inspectorate of Constabulary (1992) *Equal opportunities in the police service* (London: Home Office).

Her Majesty's Inspectorate of Constabulary. (1993) *Thematic inspection on equal opportunities* (Edinburgh: Scottish Office).

Her Majesty's Inspectorate of Constabulary (1996) *Developing diversity in the police service* (London: Home Office).

Hilton, J. (1976) 'Women in the police service', *Police Review*, 17 September, pp. 1166–70.

Ho, Loon Geok. (1974) 'History of the women police in the Singapore police force', *Singapore Journal*, January, pp. 48–52.

Hoffmann, F. (1986) 'Sexual harassment in academia; feminist theory and institutional practice', *Harvard Educational Review*, 56, pp. 105–121

Hofstede, G. (1980) *Cultural consequences: international differences in work related values* (Beverly Hills: Sage).

Holdaway, S. (1996) *The racialisation of British policing* (London: Macmillan).

Holdaway, S. and Parker (1997) 'Equal opportunities in South Yorkshire Police: a report'. University of Sheffield.

Holdaway, S, and Parker, S. (1998) 'Policing women police: uniform, patrol, promotion and representation in the CID,' *British Journal of Criminology*, 38, pp. 40–60.

Horn, R. (1996) 'Negotiating research access to organisations', *The Psychologist*, 9, pp. 551–4.

Hunt, J. (1984) 'The development of rapport through the negotiation of gender in fieldwork among police', *Human Organisations*, 43(4).

Hunt, J. (1990) 'The logic of sexism among police', *Women and Criminal Justice*, 2, pp. 3–30.

Igbinovia, P. E. (1987) 'African women in contemporary law enforcement', *Police Studies*, 10, pp. 31–5.

Jacobs, P. (1988) 'Stress among female police officers: the times are they a changing?' Paper presented at the Meeting of the Academy of Criminal Justice Sciences, San Francisco.

Jago, A. and Vroom, V. (1982) 'Sex differences in the incidence and evaluation of participative leader behaviour', *Journal of Applied Psychology*, 67, pp. 776–83.

Janoff-Bulman, R. (1988) 'Victims of violence', in Fisher, S. and Reason, J. (eds) *Handbook of life stress, cognition and health* (Chichester: Wiley).

Janus, S., Janus, C., Lord, L. and Power, T. (1988) 'Women in police work; Annie Oakley or Little Orphan Annie?', *Police Studies*, 11, pp. 124–7.

Jefferson, T. and Carlen, P. (eds) (1996) 'Masculinities, Social Relations and Crime', *British Journal of Criminology*, 36(3), Special Issue.

Johnson, L. Boulin (1991) 'Job strain among police officers: gender comparisons', *Police Studies*, 14, pp. 12–16.

Jones, S. (1986) *Policewomen and equality* (London: Macmillan).

Jones, S. (1987a) 'Making it work: some reflections on the Sex Discrimination Act', *Police Journal*, 60, pp. 294–302.

Jones, S. (1987b) 'Policewomen; caught in the Act', *Policing*, 2, pp. 129–40.

Jones, T., Newburn, T. and Smith, D. J. (1994) *Democracy and policing* (London: Policy Studies Institute).

Jordon, T., Mallindine, C. and Glasner, A. (1994) *Incidence, perceived deterrents to reporting and some possible avenues of support for women students experiencing sexual offences* (Oxford: Oxford Brookes University).

Joyce, K. (1991) 'Women in policing; an analysis of senior officers' views'. MA Dissertation, Guildford: University of Surrey.

Kanter, R. M. (1977) 'Some effects of proportions on group life: skewed sex ratios and responses to token women', *American Journal of Sociology*, 82, pp. 965–90.

Kay, S. (1994) 'Why women don't apply to become police officers', *Police Chief*, 91(9), pp. 44–5.

Kenna, R, and Sutherland, I. (1998) *In custody: a companion to Strathclyde police museum* (Glasgow: Strathclyde Police in association with Clutha Books).

Kennedy, D. B. and Homant, R. J. (1981) 'Nontraditional role assumption and the personality of the policewoman', *Journal of Police Science and Administration*, **9**(3), pp. 346–55.

Kennedy, H. (1993) 'Violence, women and the law'. Paper presented as the James Smart Lecture, Strathclyde Police Headquarters, Glasgow 29 October.

Kersten, J. (1996) 'Culture, masculinities and violence against women', *British Journal of Criminology*, 36, pp. 381–395.

Kinsley Lord (1994) *Development of an equal opportunities strategy [for] the Metropolitan Police Service* (London: Kinsley Lord Management Consultants).

Koch, U. (1998) 'Policing in the context of changing state functions: examples from Germany'. Paper presented to the 2nd International Conference Policing in Central Europe and Eastern Europe; Organizational, Managerial, and Human Resource Aspects. Ljubljana.

Kroes, W. (1982) 'Job stress in policewomen: an empirical study', *Police Stress*, Winter, pp. 10–11.

Laight, E. (1996) 'The gentle touch? The portrayal of female police officers in fictional television programmes'. BSc Dissertation. University of Portsmouth.

Lanier M. (1996) 'An evolutionary typology of women police officers', *Women and Criminal Justice*, **8** (2), pp. 35–57.

Ledwith, S. and Colgan, F. (eds) (1996) *Women in organisations: challenging gender politics* (London: Macmillan).

Lees, S. (1997) *Ruling passions: sexual violence, reputation and the law* (Buckingham: Open University Press).

Leishman, F. (1999) 'Policing in Japan: East Asian Archetype?' in Mawby, R. (ed.) *Policing Across the World.*

Lent, R. W. and Brown, S. D. (1996) 'Social cognitive approach to career development; an overview', *Career Development Quarterly*, **44**, pp. 310–21.

Leonard, D. A., Moore, C., Bowron, M. and Mertl, J. V. (1991) 'A preliminary review of policing problems, organisational requirements and training needs in the Czech and Slovack Republics'. Lewes: Sussex Police.

Lersch, K. M. (1998) 'Exploring gender differences in citizen allegations of misconduct; an analysis of a Municipal police department', *Women and Criminal Justice*, **9**, pp. 69–79.

Lester, D., Gronau, F. and Wondrack, K. (1982) 'The personality and attitudes of female police officers; needs, androgeny, and attitudes towards rape', *Journal of Police Science and Administration*, **10**, pp. 357–60.

Levine, P. (1994) 'Walking the streets in a way no decent woman should: women police in World War I', *Journal of Modern History*, **66**, pp. 34–78.

Little, C. (1996) Paper contributed to 'Cult of Masculinity' seminar at the International Association of Women Police/European Network of Policewomen Training Conference Birmingham.

Lock, J. (1979) *The British policewoman: her story* (London: Hale).

Long, B. C. (1989) 'Sex-role orientation, coping strategies, and self efficacy of women in traditional and non traditional occupations', *Psychology of Women Quarterly*, **13**, pp. 307–24.

Lord, L. K. (1986) 'A comparison of male and female peace officers' stereotypic perceptions of women and women peace officers', *Journal of Police Science and Administration*, **14**, pp. 83–97.

Love, K., and Singer, M. (1988) 'Self efficacy, psychological well being, job satisfaction and job involvement: a comparison of male and female police officers', *Police Studies*, **11**, pp. 98–102.

Loveday, B. (1996) 'Crime at the core?' in Leishman, F., Loveday, B., and Savage, S. (eds.) *Core issues in policing* (London: Longman).

Lucas, N. (1986) *WPC Courage* (London: Weidenfeld and Nicolson).

Lunneborg, P. W. (1989) *Women police officers: current career profile* (Springfield, Il: Charles C. Thomas).

MacKinnon, C. A. (1995) 'Sexual harassment: its first decade in court', in Raffel Price, B. and Sokoloff, N. (eds) *The criminal justice system and women offenders victims and co-workers*, 2nd edn (New York: McGraw-Hill).

Macpherson, Sir W. (1999) *Stephen Lawrence Inquiry*, Cm 4262–I.

McVeigh, R. (1994) 'It's part of life here: the security forces and harassment in Northern Ireland', Belfast Committee on Administration of Justice.

Mahajan, A. (1982) *Indian policewomen* (New Delhi: Deep and Deep).

Maniloff, M. (1998) 'Policewomen in France', *European Network of Policewomen Newletter*, June, pp. 2–5.

Manuel, L. L., Retzlaff, P. and Sheehan, E. (1993) 'Policewomen's personality', *Journal of Social Behavior and Personality*, **8** (1), pp. 149–53.

Marshall, I. H. (1998) 'Operation of the criminal justice system', in Kangaspunta, K., Joutsen, M. and Ollus, N. (eds) *Crime and criminal justice systems in Europe and North America 1990–1994* (Helsinki: European Institite for Crime Prevention and Control).

Marshall, P. (1973) 'Policewomen on patrol', *Manpower*, October, pp. 15–20.

Martin, C. (1996) 'The impact of equal opportunities policies on the day to day experiences of women police constables', *British Journal of Criminology*, **36**, pp. 510–28.

Martin, C. A., McKean, H. E. and Veltkramp, L. J. (1986) 'Post traumatic stress disorder in police working with victims: a pilot study', *Journal of Police Science and Administration*, **14**, pp. 98–101.

Martin, S. E. (1979) 'POLICEwomen and police WOMEN: occupational role dilemmas and choices of female officers', *Journal of Police Science and Administration*, **2**, pp. 314–23.

Martin, S. E. (1980) *Breaking and entering* (Berkeley: University of California Press).

Martin, S. E. (1989a) 'Women in policing: the 80s and beyond', in Kenney, D. (ed.) *Police and policing: contemporary issues* (New York: Praeger), pp. 3–16.

Martin, S. E. (1989b) 'Female officers on the move? A status report on women in policing', in Dunham, R. G. and Alpert, G. P. (eds) *Minorities in policing* (Prospects Heights, Il: Waveland).

Martin, S. E. (1990) *On the move: the status of women in policing* (Washington: Police Foundation).

Martin, S. E. and Jurik, N. C. (1996) *Doing justice doing gender: women in Law and Criminal Justice occupations* (Thousand Oaks, CA: Sage).

Masters, G. and Smith, D. (1998) 'Portia and Persephone revisilted: thinking about feeling in criminal justice', *Theoretical Criminology*, **2**, pp. 5–27.

Mawby, R. (1990) *Comparative policing issues: the British and American experience in international perspective* (London: Routledge).

Mawby, R. (1992) 'Comparative police systems: searching for a continental model . . .' in Bottomley, K. *et al.* (ed.) *Criminal justice: theory and practice* (London: British Society of Criminology).

Mawby, R. I. (ed.) (1999a) *Policing across the world* (London: UCL Press).

Mawby, R. (1999b) 'Approaches to comparative analysis: The impossibility of becoming an expert on everywhere', in Mawby, R. (ed.) *Policing across the ward*.

Mawby, R. (1999c) 'Variations on a theme: the development of professional police in the british isles and North America', in Mawby, R. (ed.) *Policing Across the World*.

McCullagh, C. (1996) *Crime in Ireland: a sociological introduction* (Cork: Cork University Press).

McKenzie, I. (1993) 'Equal opportunities in policing: a comparative examination of anti-discriminatory policy and practice in British policing', *International Journal of Sociology and Law*, **21**, pp. 159–74.

McKenzie, I. and Gallagher, G. P. (1989) *Behind the uniform: policing in Britain and America* (Hemel Hempstead: Harvester Wheatsheaf).

McLaughlin, E. (1992) 'The democratic deficit: European Union and the accountability of the British police', *British Journal of Criminology*, **32**(4), pp. 473–87.

Meagher, M. S. and Yentes, N. A. (1986) 'Choosing a career in policing: a comparison of male and female perceptions', *Journal of Police Science and administration*, **14**, pp. 321–7.

Melchionne, T. (1974) 'The changing role of policewomen', *Police Journal*, **XLVII**, pp. 340–58.

Messerschmidt, J. W. (1993) *Masculinities and crime: critique and reconceptualisation of theory* (Lanham. MD: Rowman and Littlefield).

Messerschmidt, J. W. (1995) 'From patriarchy to gender: feminist theory, criminology and the challenge of diversity' in Hahn Rafter, N. and Heidensohn, F. M. (eds) *International feminist perspectives in criminology* (Buckingham: Open University Press).

Mezey, G. and Rubenstein, M. (1992) 'Sexual harassment: the problem and its consequences, *Journal of Forensic Psychiatry*', **3**, pp. 221–33.

Mezey, G. and Taylor, P. (1988) 'Psychological reactions of women who have been raped; a descriptive and comparative study', *British Journal of Psychiatry*, **152** pp. 330–9.

Miller, L. and Braswell, M. (1992) 'Police perceptions of ethical decision making: the ideal vs the real', *American Journal of Police*, **XI** pp. 27–45.

Miller, S. L. (ed) (1998) *Crime control and women: feminist implications of criminal justice policy* (Thousand Oaks CA: Sage).

Mitchell, D. (1966) *Women on the warpath* (London: Jonathan Cape).

Mitchell, S. (1975) 'The policeman's wife: urban and rural', *Police Journal*, **XLVIII**, pp. 79–88.

Moore, D. B. (1994) 'Views at the top down under; Australian police managers on Australian policing', *Policing and Society*, 4, pp. 191–217.

Moore, P. J. (1992) 'An examination of the use of language in a police staff appraisal system'. MA Dissertation, University of Exeter.

Morash, M. and Greene, J. (1986) 'Evaluating women on patrol', *Evaluation Review*, **10** pp. 230–55.

Morris, A. (1987) *Women, crime and criminal justice* (Oxford: Blackwell).

Natarajan, M. (1994) 'A comparative analysis of women policing in India', *International Journal of Comparative and Applied Criminal Justice*, **18**, pp. 54–61.

Natarajan, M. (1996) 'Women police units in India: a new direction', *Police Studies*, **19**, pp. 63–75.

Neidig, P. H., Russell, H. E. and Seng, A. F. (1992) 'Interspousal aggression in law enforcement families: a preliminary investigation', *Police Studies*, **15**, pp. 30–8.

Nelken, D. (ed.) (1994) *The futures of criminology* (London: Sage).

Nelken, D. (1997) 'Understanding criminal justice comparatively' in Maguire, M. *et al.* (eds) *The Oxford handbook of criminology*, 2nd edn (Oxford: Clarendon Press).

Nevill, D. D. and Schlecker, D. I. (1988) 'The relation of selfefficacy and assertiveness to willingness to engage in traditional/nontraditional career activities', *Psychology of Women Quarterly*, **12**, pp. 91–8.

Newburn, T. (1999) *Understanding and preventing police corruption: lessons from literature*. Police Research Series paper 110, (London: Home Office).

Newburn, T. and Stanko, E. (eds) (1994) *Just boys doing business: men, masculinity and crime* (London: Routledge).

Nixon, C. (1992) 'A climate of change: police response to rape', in Breckenridge, J. and Carmody, M. (eds) *Crime of violence: Australia's responses to rape and child sexual assault* (Sydney: Allen and Unwin).

O'Kelly, D. (1959) *Salute to the Gardai 1922–1958* (Dublin: Parkside Press).

O'Mahony, P. (1996) *Criminal chaos: 7 crises in Irish criminal justice* (Dublin: Round Hall, Sweet and Maxwell).

Ott, E. Marlies (1989) 'Effects of the male–female ratio at work', *Psychology of Women Quarterly*, **13**, pp. 41–57.

Owings, C. (1925) *Women police: a study of the development and status of women police movement* (New York: Bureau of Social Hygiene).

Paddison, L. (1992) 'Halford: tip of the iceberg?', *Personnel Management*, September 6.

Paleolog, S. (n.d.) *The women police of Poland (1925 to 1939)* (London: Association for Moral and Social Hygiene).

Pendergrass, V. E, and Ostrove, N. M. (1984) 'A survey of stress in women in policing', *Journal of Police Science and Administration*, 12, pp. 303–309.

Pierce, J. (1995) *Gender trials: emotional lives in contemporary law firms* (Berkeley: University of California Press).

Pogrebin, M. (1986) 'The changing role of women: female officers' occupational problems', *Police Journal*, **59**(2), pp. 127–33.

Pollard, C. (1997) 'Zero tolerance: short term fix, long term liability?', in Dennis, N. (ed.) *Zero tolerance: policing a free society* (London: IEA Health and Welfare Unit).

Pollitz, Worden, A. (1993) 'The attitudes of women and men in policing: testing conventional and contemporary wisdom', *Criminology*, **31**, pp. 203–41

Poole, E. D. and Pogrebin, M. R. (1988) 'Factors affecting the decision to remain in the police: a study of women officers', *Journal of Police Science and Administration*, **116**, pp. 46–55.

Pope, K. E. and Pope, D. W. (1986) 'Attitudes of male police officers towards their female counterparts', *Police Journal*, **LVIX**(3), pp. 242–50.

Prenzler, T. (1992) 'Women and policing: policy implications from the US experience'. Research and Policy Paper 3, Griffith University Centre for Crime Policy and Public Safety.

Prenzler, T. (1994) 'Women in Australian policing: an overview', *Journal of Australian Studies*, **42**, pp. 78–88.

Prenzler, T. (1996) 'Rebuilding the walls? The impact of police pre-entry physical ability tests on female applicant'. Paper presented to the First Australasian Women Police Conference, Sydney 29–31 July.

Prenzler, T. (1998) 'Gender integration in Australian policing: the evolution of management responsibility', *International Journal of Police Science and Management*, pp. 1241–59.

Prenzler, T. and Wimshurst, K. (1997) 'Blue tunics and batons: women and politics in the Queensland police 1970–1987', *Journal of Australian Studies*, **52**, pp. 88–101.

Price, B. R. (1974) 'A study of leadership strength of female police executives', *Journal of Police Science and Administration*, **2**, pp. 219–26.

Price, B. R. (1989) 'Is policework changing as a result of women's contribution?' Paper presented to the International Conference on Police Women, Netherlands, 19–23 March.

Pym, P. A. (n.d.) 'Perceptions of promotion survey extract'. Devon and Cornwall Constabulary unpublished report.

Radford, J. (1989) 'Women and policing: contradictions old and new', in Hanner, J., Radford, J. and Stanko, E. (eds) *Woman, policing and male violence* (London: Macmillan), p. 12–45.

Rafter, Hahn, N. and Heidensohn, F. (eds) (1995) *International feminist perspectives in criminology – engendering a discipline* (Buckingham: Open University Press).

Rafter, N. and Heidensohn, F. (1995) 'Introduction: The development of feminist perspectives in criminology' in Rafter, N. and Heidensohn, F. (eds). *Engendering criminology: the transformation of a social science* (Milton Keynes: Open University Press).

Rawlings, P. (1995) 'The view of policing: a history', *Policing and Society*, 5, pp. 129–49.

Redshaw, J. (1994) 'Equal opportunities and the grievance procedure; an investigation into knowledge and understanding'. Devon and Cornwall Police unpublished report.

Reiner, R. (1986) *The politics of the police* (Brighton: Harvester Wheatsheaf).

Reiner, R. (1997) 'Policing and the police' in Maguire, M. *et al.* (eds.) *Oxford handbook of criminology*, 2nd edn (Oxford: Oxford University Press).

Remmington P. W. (1983) 'Women in the police: integration or separation', *Qualitative Sociology*, **6**, pp. 118–35.

Rinsema, S. (1996) 'Equal pay/equal treatment: equal pay of policewomen in the European Union'. Utrecht: University of Utrecht Research Information Centre.

Ryan, J., Ryan, M. and Ward, T. (1990) 'Feminism, philanthropy and social control: the origins of women's policing in England', in Rolston, B. and Tomlinson, M. (eds) *Gender, sexuality and social control*. The European Group for the Study of Deviance and Social Control Working Paper 10.

Salisbury, J., Ginorio, A., Remick, H. and Stringer, D. (1986) 'Counselling victims of sexual harassment', *Psychotherapy*, **23**, p. 318.

Sarkozi, I. (1994) 'Policewomen in Hungary' (Budapest: Institute for Law Enforcement Management training and Research) mimeo.

Saulsbury, W., Mott, J. and Newburn, T. (eds.) (1996) *Themes in contemporary policing* (London: Independent Committee of Inquiry into the role and responsibilities of the police).

Saunders, J. E. (1992) 'Does equality exist in the employment of women in the police service?'. Suffolk Constabulary unpublished report.

Schulz, D. (1995a) *From social worker to crime fighter* (Westport, CT: Praeger).

Schulz, D. (1995b) 'Invisible no more: a social history of women in policing', in Raffell Price, B. and Sokoloff, N. (eds) *The criminal justice system and women*, 2nd edn (New York: McGraw Hill).

Schulz, D. (1998) 'Bridging boundaries: United States policewomen's efforts to form an international network', *International Journal of Police Science and Management*, **1**(1), pp. 70–80.

Scott, A. (1997) 'Promotion in the police service: the significance of gender'. Dissertation submitted to the University of Portsmouth.

Segrave, K. (1995) *Police women: a history* (London: McFarland).

Sewell, J. (1985) *Police: Policing urban Canada* (Toronto: Lorrimer).

Shelley, L. (1999) 'Post socialist policing: limitations on institutional change' in Mawby, R. (ed.) *Policing Across the World*.

Sheptycki, J. W. E. (1995a) 'Transnational policing and the makings of the postmodern state', *British Journal of Criminology*, **35**, pp. 613–35.

Sheptycki, J. W. E. (1995b) 'Folk perils and Eurocops: criminological problems and prospects for understanding transnational crime and policing in europe'. Paper delivered at British Criminology Conference, Loughborough.

Sherman, L. J. (1975) 'An evaluation of policewomen on patrol in a suburban police department', *Journal of Police Science and Administration*, **3**, pp. 434–8.

Sherman, L. (1977) 'Policewomen around the world', *International Review of Criminal Policy*, **33**, pp. 25–33.

Siegal, D. (1992) *Sexual harassment: research and resources*, in Hallgarth, S. and Capej, M. (eds) (New York: National Council for Research on Women).

Silvestri, M. (1998) 'Visions of the future: the role of senior policewomen as agents of change', *International Journal of Police Science and Management*, **1**, pp. 148–61.

Singer, M. S. and Love, K. (1988) 'Gender differences in self perception of occupational efficacy: a study of law enforcement officers', *Journal of Social Behaviour and Personality*, **3**, pp. 63–74.

Skolnick, J. (1966) *Justice without trial* (New York: Wiley).

Smart, C. (1977) *Women, crime and criminology* (London: Routledge).

Smith, D. and Gray, J. (1985) *Police and people of London: the PSI report* (Aldershot: Gower).

Smith, James, D. (1993) 'How they sank Halford', *Sunday Times Magazine*, 23 May.

Smith, P. B., and Bond, M. H. (1993) *Social psychology across cultures*, 2nd edn (London: Prentice-Hall).

Sokoloff, N. J., Raffell-Price, B. and Kuleshnyk, I. (1992) 'A case study of black and white women police in an urban police department', *Justice Professional*, **6**, 68–85.

Southgate, P. (1981) 'Women in the police', *Police Journal*, **54**(2), 157–67.

Stalker, J. (1988) *Stalker* (Harmondsworth: Penguin).

Stanko, E. A. (1985) *Intimate intrusions* (London: Unwin Hyman).

Stanko, E. A. (1992) 'The case of fearful women: gender, personal safety and fear of crime', *Women and Criminal Justice*, **4**, pp. 117–35.

Starcevic, A. (1993) 'The un-gentle touch: the definition and coping mechanisms used by women police officers when dealing with sexual harassment'. MA Dissertation, University of Leicester.

Steel, B. S. and Loverich, N. (1987) 'Equality and efficiency trade-offs in affirmative action: real or imagined? The case of women in policing', *Social Science Research Journal*, **24**, pp. 53–70.

Stockdale, J. (1991) 'Sexual harassment at work', in Firth-Cozens, J. and West, M. (eds) *Women at work: psychological and organizational perspectives* (Milton Keynes: Open University Press).

Stuart, C. (1994) 'Harmony in diversity', *Professional Management*, 10–11 November.

Subhan, A. (ed.) (1996) *Central and Eastern European Women: a portrait* (European Parliament: Directorate General for Planning).

Sutton, J. (1996) 'Women of the New South Wales Police'. Paper presented to the First Australasian Women Police Conference. Sydney, 29–31 July.

Sutton, J. (1992) 'Women in the job', in Moir, P. and Eijkman, H. (eds) *Policing Australia: old issues, new perspectives* (Melbourne: Macmillan).

Tancred, E. (n.d.) 'Women police 1914–1950'. National Council of women of Great Britain.

Tancred, E. (1941) *Some notes on the progress of women police* (London: National Council for Women).

Taylor, C. and McKenzie, I. (1994) 'The glass ceiling at the top of the greasy pole', *Policing*, 10, pp. 260–7.

Tempest, G. (1993) 'Equal opportunities survey [in the] North Yorkshire Police'. Unpublished report.

Toch, H. (1976) *Peacekeeping, police, prison and violence* (Lexinton, MA: Lexington Books).

Trzcinska, W. (1996) 'Women in Polish police: facts against myths', *ENP Newsletter*, 2 August, pp. 2–3.

Tynan, M. (1995) '80 years of women in policing New South Wales 1915–1995'. Sydney NSW Police Service.

Van Dijk, J. J. M. (1997) 'Determinants of crime', in Kangaspunta, K., Joutsen, M. and Ollus, N. (eds) *Crime and criminal justice systems in Europe and North America 1990–1994* (Helsinki: European Institite for Crime Prevention and Control).

Van Wormer, K. (1980) 'Are males suited to police patrol work?', *Police Studies*, 3 pp. 41–4.

Vega, M. and Silverman, I. J. (1982) 'Female police officers as viewed by their male counterparts', *Police Studies*, 5 pp. 31–9.

Waddington, P. A. J. (1999) 'Police (canteen) culture; an appreciation', *British Journal of Criminology*, 39 pp. 287–309.

Walker, M. (1997) 'Conceptual and methodological issues in the investigation of occupational stress: a case study of police officers deployed on body recovery at the site of the Lockerbie air crash', *Policing and Society*, 7, pp. 1–17.

Walker, S. G. (1993) 'The status of women in Canadian policing'. Solicitor General Ministry Secretariat. Report no. 1933–22.

Walklate, S. (1992) 'Jack and Jill join up at Sunhill: public images of police officers', *Policing and Society*, 2 pp. 219–32.

Walklate, S. (1993) 'Policing by women, with women, for women?' *Policing*, 9, pp. 101–15.

Walklate, S. (1995) 'Equal opportunities and the future of policing', in Leishman, F. Loveday, B. and Savage S. (eds) *Core issues in policing* (London: Longman).

Water, J. van de (1987) 'Wat gebeurt er met vrouwen in de opleiding en tijdens de stage-periode van diezelfde opleiding en de hoeverre heert dit aanknopingspunten met de theorie?' Dissertation, University of Utrecht.

Watson, S. (1992). 'Femocratic feminism', in Savage, M. and Witz, A. (eds) *Gender and Bureaucracy* (Oxford: Blackwells).

Waugh, A. (1994) 'A case study of policewomen's experience in New Zealand'. MSc Dissertation, University of Wellington.

Waugh, L., Ede, A. and Alley, A. (1998) 'Police culture and attitudes towards misconduct', *International Journal of Police Science and Management*, 1, pp. 288–300.

Weigel. E. (1991) 'Schutzfrau in der mannerwelt', *Deutsche Polizei*, **4**, pp. 4–7.

Weinberger, B. (1993) 'A policewife's lot is not a happy one: police wives in the 1930s and 1940s', *Oral History*, Autumn, pp. 46–53.

Weinberger, B. (1995) *The best police in the world: an oral history of English policing from 1930s to the 1960s* (Aldershot: Scolar Press).

Weisheit, R. A. (1987) 'Women in the state police: concerns of male and female officers', *Journal of Police Science and Administration*, **15**(2), pp. 137–44.

Wertsch, T. L. (1998) 'Walking the thin blue line: policewomen and tokenisin today', *Women and Criminal Justice*, **9**, pp. 23–61.

Westmarland, L. (1994) 'An investigation into possible barriers to equal opportunities for women in Durham Constabulary'. University of Durham, Department of Sociology and Social Policy. Unpublished report.

Wexler, J. G. and Logan, D. D. (1983) 'Sources of stress among women police officers', *Journal of Police Science and Administration*, **11**, pp. 46–53.

Wexler, J. G. and Quinn, V. (1985) 'Considerations in the training and development of women sergeants', *Journal of Police Science and Administration*, **13**, pp. 98–105.

Whitaker, B. (1979) *Police in society* (London: Eyre Methuen).

Wilkie, R. and Currie, C. (1989) *The effects of sex discrimination on the Scottish police service* (Strathclyde: University of Strathclyde Centre for Police Studies).

Wilkinson, J., and Campbell, E. A. (1997) *Psychology in counselling and therapeutic practice* (Chichester: Wiley).

Wilkinson, V. and Froyland, I. D. (1996) 'Women in policing', *Australian Institute of Criminology Trends and Issues in Crime and Criminal Justice*, **58**, pp. 1–6.

Wimshurst, K. (1995) 'Anticipating the future: the early experiences and career expectations of women police recruits in post Fitzgerald Queensland', *Australian and New Zealand Journal of Criminology*, **28**, pp. 278–97.

Women's Advisory Council to the Los Angeles Police Commission (1993) 'A blueprint for implementing gender equity in the Los Angeles Police Department'. Unpublished report.

Woodeson, A. (1993) 'The first women police: a force for equality or infringement?' *Women's History Review*, **2**, pp. 217–32.

Worden, Pollitz, A. (1993) 'The attitudes of women and men in policing: testing conventional and contemporary wisdom', *Criminology*, **31**, pp. 203–41.

Wurz, J. (1993) *Frauen in vollzugsdienst der schutzpolizei. Europaische Hochschulschriften* (Frankfurt am Main: Peter Lang).

Wyles, L. (1951) *A woman at Scotland Yard* (London: Faber).

Yang, J. (1981) 'Women in policing; a comparative study of the United States and the Republic of China (Taiwan)', *Police Studies*, **8**, pp. 125–31.

Young, M. (1984) 'Police wives', in Callan, H. and Ardener, S. (eds) *Incorporated wives* (London: Croom Helm).

Youngblood, S. (1993) 'After all these years have men accepted women police officers?' *Womenpolice*, 27, 2, pp. 15–16.

Young, M. (1991) *Inside job* (Oxford: Clarendon).

Zvekic, U. (1998) *Criminal victimisation in countries in transition* (Rome: UNICRI).

Index